JAMAICA KINCAID'S PRISMATIC SUBJECTS: MAKING SENSE OF BEING IN THE WORLD

For Mark and Micol

JAMAICA KINCAID'S PRISMATIC SUBJECTS:

MAKING SENSE OF BEING IN THE WORLD

by

Giovanna Covi

MANGO PUBLISHING
2003

First published 2003

Published by Mango Publishing, London UK
P.O. Box 13378, London SE27 OZN
email: info@mangoprint.com
website: www.mangoprint.com

ISBN 1 902294 24 6

British Library Cataloguing in Publication Data
A CIP catalogue record for this book is available from the British Library

Printed in the Print Solutions Partnership

Contents

NOTE
References to Jamaica Kincaid's works discussed in this study are given parenthetically
in the text with the following abbreviations:
BR   *At the Bottom of the River*, New York: Farrar, Straus and Giroux, 1983
AJ   *Annie John*, New York: Farrar, Straus and Giroux, 1986
SP   *A Small Place*, New York: Farrar, Straus and Giroux, 1988
'O'   'Ovando' in *Conjunctions* 14 (1989): 75-83
'SE'   'On Seeing England for the First Time' in *Transition* 51 (1991): 32-40
L   *Lucy*, New York: Farrar, Straus and Giroux, 1990
A   *The Autobiography of My Mother*, New York: Farrar, Straus and Giroux, 1996
MB   *My Brother,* New York: Farrar, Straus and Giroux, 1997
MG   *My Garden (Book):*, New York: Farrar, Straus and Giroux, 1999
MP   *Mr. Potter*, New York: Farrar, Straus and Giroux, 2002

ACKNOWLEDGMENTS

In the Spring of 2000, a Research Associateship at the Beatrice Bain Center for Women's Studies, University of California at Berkeley, allowed me the opportunity to complete research for this study. I am particularly grateful to Gee Gee Lang for her generous assistance.

This publication is supported by a grant from the Dipartimento di Scienze Filologiche e Storiche of the Università degli Studi di Trento.

Introduction

In the Company of Jamaica Kincaid's Prismatic Subjects

My interpretation of Jamaica Kincaid is inspired by the conviction that, as a feminist, I must always articulate a gendered position which should be accessible not only across disciplines but hopefully also outside the academic context. I militantly subscribe to this commitment, although I am conscious of my inevitable failures to achieve this goal. I am aware, as well, that despite my firm belief that culture and socio-politics are strictly interrelated, it is rare to see change in cultural discourse produce immediate and direct effects on our socio-political reality.

This critical project is shaped by my determination to attempt to dismantle, through a rhetorical stance as well as by means of my conceptual interpretation, the boundaries which separate theory from practice in politics, and divide philosophy from poetry in culture, in the hope that intellectual activity does not risk becoming divorced from moral concerns. As Gayatri Spivak puts it, 'to theorize the political, to politicize the theoretical, are such vast aggregative asymmetrical undertakings; the hardest lesson is the impossible intimacy of the ethical.'[1] Much has been written, especially in feminist terms, about questioning this border, but critical theory is still too widely framed in terms which present its concepts as if they were a metaphysical system within which to fit, and under which to subsume the object of study — the literary text. As a critic, my struggle is to keep the agency of literature alive and avoid subsuming the text to my theory. In other words, this study is ambitiously aimed at placing Jamaica Kincaid within feminist discourse in order to transform the latter and give to our contemporary understanding as a whole a permeable cognitive frame by which interaction, change, dialogue, interruption, and even contradiction are included to develop the potential for inhabiting a world in which different cultures can enjoy equal citizenship. I would like this choice to contribute to an empowering re-definition of contemporary culture as a discourse capable of expressing differences which make a difference within the intricate network of global power that determines our social existence.

Since 1983, Kincaid's narratives have provided the cognitive tools to help me make sense of my own being in this world — they have given to me what Marie Cardinal would call 'the words to say it.'[2] The purpose of this study is to try to show the extent to which a woman writer claiming an African and a Carib Indian identity, a US resident who for decades has never renounced her Antiguan citizenship, and who consistently embraces a point of view which includes the Antiguan perspective while accounting for her transnational location, can contribute to enhancing richness, complexity, even justice and democracy in a globalized context, rather than resting on the easily marketable levelling of all differences into a wider and re-vamped culture of the melting pot. Accepting the temporality of being, the worldliness of our existential condition — to put it loosely in Heideggerian terms — implies also grounding our definition of identity on the changing socio-historical context. Jamaica Kincaid uncompromisingly rejects the violence and discrimination inflicted upon the larger part of the world by a globalized economy, but in doing so she does not shy away from 'rethinking thinking,'[3] thus contributing incisively to the creation of a transnational culture capable of travelling across borders and of speaking to the widest possible constituency. This achievement is exemplified by the script *Life and Debt*,[4] Kincaid's re-writing for video of her own *A Small Place* (1988), in which she transfers her original story from Antigua to Jamaica in the same pointed denunciation of the IMF: through Kincaid's narration, the video powerfully demonstrates that the subaltern[5] — Jamaica in this case — can be represented without being fossilized into alterity.

While I was first struggling with the conjugation of feminism, marxism and postmodernism — what I liked to call a postmodernist feminism of resistance[6] — Kincaid's *At the Bottom of the River* (1983) provided me with a tangible figuration of subjectivity contextualized in terms that joined the force of political thinking with the beauty of lyrical speaking. She did so by offering the metaphor of a prism, which I have since borrowed to make sense of a positioning which struggles to be located, relational, and intercultural:

'I stood as if I were a prism, many-sided and transparent, refracting and reflecting light as it reached me, light that never could be destroyed. And how beautiful I became' (*BR* 80).[7]

This is how a young girl figures herself as she learns to dominate her will and with this gains the strength to interact, as a self who is temporal and corporeal, with the rest of the transient world. At the bottom of the river she sees the truth of her own self-invention: the solid body of a prism, rich in the multitude of its many faces which actively act upon and are modified by the light they encounter. This body draws its will to be from its capacity to invent a world 'in which the sun and the moon [shine] at the same time' (BR 77); they do so in such unison that the various things and beings that inhabit their world stand 'not yet divided, not yet examined, not yet numbered, and not yet dead' (BR 78). This is a self whose will makes it possible to imagine life outside of the classifications imposed upon it by natural science, and outside the neat grid imposed upon it by the reason of modernity. And this imagination gives her the power to claim for herself the 'perishable and transient' nature of existence, and to 'grow solid and complete' with her 'name filling up ... [her] mouth' (BR 82). Here is a subject who powerfully chooses to identify with her own mother in a way similar to the tension articulated by Adrienne Rich,[8] rather than an identity annihilated and dissolved into the pre-Oedipal world of a Kristevan *chora*,[9] which must exclude history in order to exist poetically. Indeed, here is a subject who has become 'beautiful' (BR 80) because it has reached a beauty which, as Elaine Scarry claims, exerts pressure 'towards ethical equality.'[10] And here is also the first and inerasable figuration of a subject in continuous transformation, whose capacity to articulate critically the processes of non-linear change that characterize human life in the contemporary post-human and inhuman complexity is grounded on a materialist theory of becoming, as suggested by Rosi Braidotti in *Metamorphoses*.[11]

In 1985, *Annie John* offered to me the narrative voice of an adolescent girl who emphasizes that her prismatic body matters because it has gained the strength to perform in the world — in Eve K. Sedgwick's words, because she comes to realize the empowering force of the speech act:[12] 'My name is Annie John,' she says as she moves beyond her initial complete identification with her mother and native place. Grandmother Ma Chess, an obeah woman who magically appears and disappears in body and spirit, teaches her that a 'home' is not fixed in place like a 'house,' thus preparing her for independence and separation. Ma Chess heals Annie from depression and gets her ready to leave Antigua and her family to emigrate to England 'forever,' when she observes: 'A house?

Why live in a house? All you need is a nice hole in the ground, so you can come and go as you please' (*AJ* 126). Ma Chess's acceptance of the *Unheilimlichkeit*, the not-at-homeness of a Heideggerian *Dasein*, whose basic state is being-in-the-world, spatially and temporally, with oneself, the others and with care,[13] has helped me appreciate Gayatri Spivak's struggle to keep the poetic word united with the historical world,[14] without having to use what Rosi Braidotti calls 'the ugly language of philosophy';[15] Ma Chess has also given body to a postmodernist acceptance of displacement — the condition of a changing, relational subjectivity which does not conjugate its own inevitable estrangement with modernist anxiety, thus grounding postmodernism in the physical fact; finally and most importantly, Ma Chess has done so without confusing the historical condition of emigration with the romanticized figuration of exile.[16] Ma Chess's teaching serves as a form of empowerment for Annie's destiny, while her coming-and-going gives a deeper significance to the initial metaphor of a prismatic subjectivity and makes of *Annie John* much more than a coming-of-age story.

I hope these examples show why my enthusiasm for Jamaica Kincaid in the years 1988-90 grew into a militant passion. The illustrated book *Annie, Gwen, Lilly, Pam and Tulip* (1989)[17] provided a triumphantly graphic rendering of a relational feminist subjectivity, with five voices woven together to draw Eric Fischl's first diminished, crouched figure from darkness into his last images of bright, multi-colored, full-blown and self-assertive women: here prismatic subjectivity is made equally visible through Fischl's paintbrush and through the intimately relational female voices which echo and transform one another in the text. Here, subjectivity is also turned into powerful, beautiful agency.

Agency found then its full articulation in *Lucy* (1990), in which the protagonist shows — by writing her own full name in the final scene of the novel — that identity is also an 'invention,'[18] a process of creation (as such, an act which unites the material and the linguistic/spiritual) that is always in progress and yet, despite its linguistic origin, such creation provides a fundamental grounding for experience and social acting. The conclusion of this book has become a milestone in my own feminist theoretical meanderings:

> I wrote my full name: Lucy Josephine Potter. At the sight of it many thoughts rushed through me, but I could write down only this: 'I wish I could love someone so much that I could die from it.' And then as I

looked at this sentence a great wave of shame came over me and I wept and wept so much that the tears fell on the page and caused all the words to become one great big blur. (*L* 162-63)

Lucy has helped me to give body to the theoretical debate engaged by feminist scholars in the 1980s. With Lucy, Linda Alcoff's 'positionality within a context' has become tangible,[19] and capable of speaking as 'a dynamic process'; she has personified the subject which Teresa de Lauretis defines as being semiotically constructed through practice and experience.[20] Like Gayatri Spivak's 'questioning subject,' Lucy has appeared only 'strategically' committed to essentialism;[21] and her subjectivity, always already de-essentialized, is indeed one that 'baffles definition' and yet is defined as she assumes a definite positionality within different contexts, as Trinh T. Minh-ha suggests.[22] Lucy's strategic consciousness is kept in fluid interaction and constant motion by a practice of self-analysis, thereby her complex self, relational to a moving context, is also the locus for the construction of meaning. Lucy showed me the way out of the impasse imposed by what in the 1980s felt as the obligatory choice between either the essentialism of liberal and cultural feminists' conception of woman as a biologically grounded subject and the nominalism of poststructural feminists' rejection of the concept woman as semiotic discourse. Moreover, Lucy's 'great big blur' has provided me 'the words to say it': indeed, the conjugation of essentialist with nominalist theoretical positions, which mostly concerned me in those years during which feminism suffered from a metaphysical divide, found its solution when my understanding of the heart of the matter became translated into living as a 'big blur.' Prismatic agency by now had fully achieved complexity and knew how to inhabit space and transform it, rather than resting on a given, fixed location upon which subjectivity is supposedly rooted and imprisoned.

For instance, when Lucy rejects the modernist model of New York artists and starts writing, her stance is as subversive as, although radically different from that of the punk performing writer Kathy Acker:[23] both Lucy and Kathy scratch the surface of the gilded ghettos of the artistic avant-garde to expose its detachment from human existence. And Lucy also embraces Alice Walker's idea of the 'mothers' gardens' to displace it within the space of separation from her mother, allowing her expression no other grounding than the force coming from the acceptance of Audre

Lorde's dictum that 'poetry is not a luxury.'[24] Lucy in New York 'invents' for herself a name which is nothing other than the one she was given at birth in Antigua; she speaks in a voice that does dissolve into 'a great big blur' only after it has expressed itself clearly. By bringing the maternal into the paternal Lacanian Symbolic, by showing that identity — once posited — is unbearable and must be continuously blurred, Lucy speaks from and to a place situated beyond the dichotomy of gender opposition. This does not mean that she speaks in a mythic androgynous voice: Lucy remains a sexualized subjectivity while rejecting the reduction of multiple, fluid sexuality to the exclusionary binarism of gender.[25] Similarly, she brings 'the islands' (the Caribbean) to the metropolitan centre of the contemporary empire (New York), thus giving voice to desire. Thinking by comparison of Caliban's unexpressed desire for his own female companion, or of the 'monstrous' longing for an 'equal companion' by Dr. Frankenstein's wretched creature, I like to say that Lucy has finally given voice to these suppressed subjects and thus changed the whole narrative of alterity. Her challenging identity shakes the boundaries between subject and object and repeatedly rejects the humanistic need for external grounding; her self-presentation as 'a slight' signifier 'without substance' provides a most effective definition of the fundamental postmodern subsumption of signifiers back into the system of meaning and allows her provisional, relational 'prismatic identity' to decolonialize subjectivity and make her former-subaltern voice heard.[26] Yet, she never reduces identity to a pure play of the signifiers.

With reference to Mahasweta's fiction, Gayatri Spivak states that it 'focuses on [the subaltern] as the space of the displacement of the colonization-decolonization reversal':[27] I believe Kincaid's focus, voice and point of view deploy the same deconstructive strategy, as exemplified not only in A Small Place, where the dramatization of the native's 'I' and the tourist's 'You' complicates a mere opposition, but even more so in The Autobiography of My Mother (1996), where the narrative voice belongs to the dispossessed and makes the silenced speak. She does not give us the voice of the Other, as if it were a display in a museum, nor a new Orientalist attempt to turn the whole world into an immigrant.[28] In Spivak's critique, Lucy is poignantly described as 'a powerful paratactic text that loses nothing of its cutting edge against the exploiters, because it dares, in closing, to dissolve the central character's proper name by an alterity beyond its choice, so that it can claim, in the subjunctive, the right/responsibility of loving, denied to the subject that wishes to choose agency from victimage.'[29] How far the risk-taking acceptance of the responsibility of loving will take Kincaid's redefinition of subjectivity and collective agency is made explicit in her subsequent works.

Why then be surprised at the anger in A Small Place with which such voice interprets the world that has so dramatically discriminated against her and yet does not occupy an a-critical position? This lyrical political essay meditates upon imperial power relations throughout modernity, from colonialism to global economy, and makes it absolutely clear that the Other does not speak to enlarge the knowledge of the One, nor to increase the number of halls dedicated to 'ethnic cultures' in our natural history museums. Rather, she speaks in order to dismantle the epistemological frame that has supported not only the hierarchy but most importantly the very existence of the binarism One-Other.

A Small Place is the work of a ballad-singer, whose protest voice is enriched by a chorus that contextualizes and relativizes her rage, thus politicizing a reaction which is never allowed to withdraw into psychological confinement. The sound and word repetitions express the struggle against ideology and dogma, in a way that is no less powerful than the opposition to injustice and racism expressed by the logical organization of the discourse. Form and content constantly comment on each other, preventing the petrifaction of thought: the message is carried by a sea tide, though it is impossible to say upon which particular wave. From a relentless, sarcastic disapproval of the obtuse tourist in Antigua, addressed directly as 'you' and unequivocally shown to be associated to the colonialist,[30] the perspective turns to 'the natives' to show that they are not unblemished heroes. Looking at the history of slavery and colonization and expressing her indignation for having been forced 'to see the world through England' (SP 33), the ballad-singer uncompromisingly moves through poetry to stretch and reach the actual political fight for those cultures inhabiting the cutting edge of survival. A contrapuntal structure transmits the contradictions and injustices undergone by a colonized, enslaved people, when two narrative voices merge in a fugal stretto passage in which a focal reversal turns again on the addressee. When the story moves into the corruption of the post-colonial Antiguan government, the singer's 'rage' becomes 'bitterness and shame' (SP 41); another wave then carries an impersonal external voice (SP 51), and soon after the tide brings the intrusion of an autobiographical judgment on the people of the island, on American hegemony and the domination of multinational capital, and on Swiss neutrality (*SP* 60), completely reversing the roles assigned to the voices of the First Part.

While political and economic inter-connections are spelled out, the cultural concepts supporting them are certainly not understated and the non-logocentric development of the story strengthens its effect. But what makes Kincaid's discourse radically subversive is the fact that this speculation is solidly anchored to the historically defined situation of the 'small place' — Antigua. Thus temporal — as opposed to mythical — repetition governs both structure and theme; memory interacts with the present, rather than freezing into a nostalgic paralysis; the recurring pattern is not a litany, but a way of showing connections on a larger and larger scale. This naturally leads to the omniscient narrator of the last section focusing on the present time, in which paradox and opposites are accepted and in which the 'you' and the 'I' prismatically blur into a mutual 'human beings' (*SP* 81), because there are no longer masters to be angry at nor slaves to be proud of (*SP* 81). The oxymoronic figuration of Antigua (*SP* 78) as a prison of beauty comments upon the oxymoron of post-colonialism. Kincaid's recollection of the British colonial imperialism becomes a Foucauldian counter-memory and a ten-by-twelve-mile island becomes the focus for understanding the contemporary imperialism of the US and of global capital.

In 1998, with the historical tale 'Ovando,' and in 1991, with the fictional essay 'On Seeing England for the First Time,' Kincaid's study of the cultural implications of colonialism explore history and the centre of colonial empire in striking terms. Her study of power and powerlessness in 'Ovando' moves into the territory of the gothic genre, while in 'On Seeing England for the First Time' a female colonized voice ironically utters her rage at the discovery that the grand image held up by the masculine imperial voice to make her feel inferior was all a lie, starting with the untrue whiteness of the Cliffs of Dover.

In 1996, Jamaica Kincaid published *The Autobiography of My Mother*, whose narrator tackles the question of coming to terms with history from a theoretical point of view while asking herself, who am I in relation to others? It does so by explicitly redefining history as discourse: at the end of what she aptly calls her 'sermonette' (*A* 132-8), she offers us more than a picture with commentary of a specific socio-cultural reality; in fact, she gives us also the theory that makes that picture so devastating when she says: 'For me history was not only the past: it was the past and it was also the present' (A 138-9).

Conceiving history as discourse has broad implications on this text's portrayal of the world and of subjectivity in general. *The Autobiography* provides an exemplary model of Gayatri Spivak's concept of 'cultural translation' — a concept I extend to include a definition of feminist theory, which is always also practice. As translated subjectivity, a self is conceived as a passing entity, circulating among different contexts and never frozen into the transcendental icon of an identity. Like history, subjectivity is discursive. As such, it retains the rhetoricity of language and it works in the silent spaces between and around words. 'The jagged relation between rhetoric and logic,' Spivak points out, 'as condition and effect of knowing, allows the world to be made of an agent who acts in it in an ethical, a political, a day-to-day way.' This is why she suggests that translated thinking 'forces us to say things for which no language previously existed.'[31]

This effort to say the yet-unsaid participates in what Angela Carter calls 'decolonialization of language and thought,' a 'slow process' which helps me clarify the significance of the role played by language/rhetoric in the production of social agency and of subjectivity. Carter points out that it has nothing to do with being 'a legislator of humankind;' rather, it works towards bringing affiliations within a particular historical context through risking language and questioning logic.[32] In *The Autobiography*, translated thinking takes apart the structuring features of Modernity by uprooting the definitions of history and death. Reading *The Autobiography* as a discursive articulation of a feminist subjectivity in a specific cultural and socio-historical context, rather than as the account of a personal life, allows me to foreground not only its historical value — Xuela as a metaphorical representation of the experience of the African diaspora and of the genocide of the Carib Indians — but also its epistemological impact, its positive propositional force. Rather than the despair of the narrator's life, in Xuela I am driven to read the rejection of an Americanized cultural viewpoint that sentimentally forces happy endings upon the common hardships of life.

Explicitly and from the beginning, *The Autobiography* demands that we rid ourselves of the opposition between fact and fiction, by giving us a narration governed by 'truth' and 'invention' — a discursive elaboration of personal experience into political, theoretical knowledge, which questions the separation between fact and fiction imposed upon literature by Modern culture.[33] Toni Morrison makes it clear that a very large part of the literary heritage of Africans in the Americas is the autobiography, that 'no slave society in the history of the world wrote more — or more thoughtfully — about its own enslavement than the African-Americans'; yet, it is also true that 'they dropped a veil over things which were too terrible to relate' and thus it becomes mandatory for Morrison to integrate her memories and recollections with the force of her imagination — the only way to invent the truth.[34] *The Autobiography* is an 'invention': it is as true as the green grass and the flowers around the house with the red roof at the bottom of the river (*BR* 75-6). It is a slow process of re-memorying and decolonializing, aimed at attributing political significance to personal experience, capable of risking language and identity in order to explore new epistemic possibilities, thus allowing us to hope for a world no longer ruled by the impulse to conquer other people and control our own death.[35]

Jamaica Kincaid's brother died while she was completing *The Autobiography*; soon after, she published *My Brother* (1997), a narrative which explores the boundaries of subjectivity in its confrontation with death. The book is not only about Kincaid's brother who died of AIDS but also about the effort engaged by the author to distill her personal experience in order to make sense of death — and thus of life. This text addresses the infinitely simple, yet overwhelmingly complex question: 'if it is so certain, death, why is it such a surprise?' (*MB* 193); it elaborates the statement which shapes the story 'At the Bottom of the River' — 'Inevitable to life is death and not inevitable to death is life. Inevitable' (*BR* 72) — thus making it clear that life in all of Kincaid's writings is not the opposite of death, but that which includes it; this is why the reverse, life being inevitable to death, is not possible. Death thus is written on, and not written against. This act of dealing straightforwardly with death, certainly not a happy circumstance in itself but inescapable for all of us, is not bleak in itself but rather a propositional stance which shows the way to rid ourselves of what Wilson Harris rightly indicates as being at the roots of a history of conquest, rape, and inquisitions: namely, the impulse to conquer death, which is so pervasive as to be equated to the resurrection of Christ, in turn figured by the sorrowful mother.[36] Harris calls for a re-imagination in the form of a re-birth of epic-as-arrival, as transfiguration versus photographic description. Harris's epic voice of arrival provides one useful frame for my reading of Kincaid's relational identity.

The new epic by a prismatic voice may not tell us always what we like to hear. Indeed it upsets readers trapped in a Hollywood-like ethics of good feelings, happy endings and correct lines. Unlike the classical myth of Orpheus, Kincaid's poetic voice does not need a dead woman to whom to sing its love: its relational need would be satisfied by singing its everyday happiness to the interlocutor, Eurydice, who makes that love and the uniqueness of the lovers possible. Eurydice neither needs to be confined to the Underworld nor rescued to this one as nothing more than a pawn of Death — a liberation which would be only a fraud. There's no easy liberal nor superficially postmodern solution to the violence imposed upon the world by the individualism of the unity of the subject: no erasure of the Other nor fragmentation of both the One and the Other. 'I' and 'You' remain in their fundamental particularities and the perfect reader — present in *My Brother* as the late Mr. Shawn ('so I write about the dead for the dead,' she observes, 'but I keep writing'; *MB* 198) — reads not what he wants to hear but also things he does not like (*MB* 197). We may not like to read that 'all of us face impending death' (*MB* 102), but in the face of this reality I find it imperative to be able to narrate, as Kincaid does, even though writing at times must be 'about the dead for the dead.'

It is only to Western listeners, Harrison again observes, that the Carib Indians' flute made of human bone could evoke a cannibalistic act. Rather, its music expresses a void which is an inner presence and which our imagination is invited to fill in unexpected ways.[37] Kincaid's lyrical theory changes our epistemological and ontological boundaries and relates existence to the mother — rather than grounding it in the mother's womb and instead of envisioning it as an impossible transcendental struggle against death. It does so while fully accepting that subjectivity takes shape in the narrative — it is a true invention. According to Rikki Ducornet, 'the capacity for invention makes the world worth wanting.'[38]

For me Kincaid's capacity for invention has made her works worth reading over these years; most importantly, her continuous re-writings of the culture 'on the run' of prismatic subjectivities in passing has given me the inspiration to invent readings which are kept 'on the run' as they are passed through and as they pass through her new stories.[39] In 1999,

Kincaid's *My Garden (Book)*, a text initially buried among manuals for gardening in bookstores that still hasn't received the theoretical attention it richly deserves, was inspired by the question, 'What to do?' and continued the prismatic subject's exploration of living conceived as a process which includes dying. It is a declaration of love for 'the rush of things' (*MG* 24), for the messiness of a living in which the moment of perfection is not isolated from what comes after and before it, for the temporality of a being which is forcefully described as being able 'to make the rational way imbued with awe' (*MG* 16), and which is incapable of separating knowledge from experience. Such being can feel joy for the process of living rather than for reaching a point of completion in living; thus she is at home in the garden — the space inhabited by continuous striving rather than final accomplishment. The garden thus re-defined — as opposed to the garden as figure of the human mastering of Nature — is the proper space of the prismatic subject, satisfied with what 'must never completely satisfy' (*MG* 220), with 'an arrangement of things carefully attended to, so that it . . . looks neglected, abandoned' (*MG* 227). Here, I suggest, the 'prism' inhabits embodied desire, and her poetics becomes a discourse of love, which is the condition for outlining Kincaid's political dream for an undivided human collectivity.[40]

I read this as a necessary step towards the latest metamorphosis of 'the prism' in *Mr. Potter* (2002). In this book, subtitled 'a novel' like *The Autobiography* even though it might be classified a memoir or biography like *My Brother*, Kincaid's writing elaborates her personal experience of having had a father who rejected his paternal responsibility when she was born. By telling the story of a man now dead who refused to acknowledge her own existence and who remained unknown to her, she launches an extreme challenge to the foundational assumption of biographical narrative; indeed, the text defiantly and repeatedly underlines that this is a biography of nobody who is becoming somebody only through writing. Kincaid profoundly deconstructs the referential realistic foundation of biography by turning this 'nobody' into somebody explicitly and solely through story-telling. Thus, through a speech act — rather, a writing act — Kincaid creates Mr. Potter so that her own prismatic subjectivity can also confront the absent father-figure who denied her an identity at the beginning of her life. Only in the pages of Kincaid's 'novel' the 'nobody' who is Mr. Potter becomes someone — an absent father. Writing therefore is again an act of telling (oneself), an endless and necessary process of auto/biography-ing which entails making sense of oneself in the attempt to make sense of the world: the prismatic subject continuously metamorphoses as she passes through life. In *Mr. Potter*, Kincaid tells how her empowered prismatic subject can elaborate also her first and most personal experience of deprivation and exclusion and is now capable of relating even to her absent father. Indeed, she is capable of making him present through her writing which is a 'making sense' (*MP* 181); she actually makes him by writing on him and by making sense of her own being in the world as she relates even to this blankness and nothingness that constitutes her own origin. Mr. Potter's nothingness clearly stands also for the silenced voices of enslaved Africans in the New World.

Because this perspective means so much and is so intimate to me, I have decided to phrase this study around the idea of being-in-the-world, as opposed to 'having a life'. In this perspective, the act of writing becomes inextricably linked to survival, and cognition is an inevitable part of experience which is always elaborated intellectually. Moreover, it is a contingent and temporal elaboration, as my discussion of Kincaid's works is meant to underline. Also the temporality of my own readings over the past twenty years is inerasable; I hope the shift of my attention, and I believe Kincaid's as well, from identity politics to a politics of inter-subjectivities expresses cultural elaborations of equally fundamental contingent and temporal importance rather than giving the unintentional impression of intellectual and artistic progress.

With the title *Jamaica Kincaid's Prismatic Subjects: Making Sense of Being in the World*, I would like to capture precisely this fundamental concept, which I view as the shaping tool of Kincaid's narratives. The First Chapter, 'Epistemic Subversions in a Caribbean Voice' discusses Jamaica Kincaid as a feminist lyrical theorist in the way I have briefly sketched out here in order to deconstruct the separation of philosophical and narrative from lyrical and poetical thinking. This chapter highlights Kincaid's exploration of Caribbean history in order to emphasize that her theoretical voice is situated in place and time. I insist on considering Jamaica Kincaid a 'theorist' as a provocative gesture to counter the tendency of Euro-US feminism to recognize philosophical skills in the North, and only ethnic difference in the South.[41] But I make it a point to treat strategically Jamaica Kincaid as a theorist — not to reduce her to a mere theorist, but rather to bring her lyrical thinking into the theoretical debate articulated by feminists engaged in a postcolonial discourse incorporating marxist and poststructuralist concerns. By trying to show the various ways Kincaid speaks to and with — rather than is explicated by — feminist scholars such as Donna Haraway, Gayatri Spivak, Chandra Mohanty, Inderpal Grewal and Caren Kaplan, as well as feminist writers such as Gloria Anzaldùa, Audre Lorde, Adrienne Rich, and Angela Carter, my stance is precisely meant to counter the separation between metropolitan academic thinkers and peripheral, ethnic poets. Spivak has helped me reject this separation in her articulation of the concept of 'worlding,' which shows how the individualist subject position is constructed by means of exclusion of 'the native woman.'[42] No less, Audre Lorde has empowered me with the words to articulate this concept in her essay 'Poetry is not a Luxury.' Kincaid's writings demonstrate that the subaltern can indeed speak, provided she creates her own poetry so that she can speak neither in the subordinate nor the hegemonic voice; the parallel necessary question thus rises: can the privileged listen and how? By putting into play these different perspectives, I struggle to position my own 'privileged' listening in such a way that my understanding may possibly avoid cooptation.

This position is articulated through a discussion of *My Garden (Book):*, which makes it crystal clear that a metaphor is a cognitive and not a linguistic entity,[43] thus giving political force to Kincaid's careful attention to language throughout her whole work. This book explores the meaning of garden (the title is structured as a dictionary entry) as an icon of colonial culture: not only the Garden of Eden, but England, the Fatherland as Eden, and the British Colony as the extension of its garden; and also the garden as botanical garden and a history of naming/possessing/domesticating large parts of the world; and finally as the image of a feminine confinement into the domestic sphere, the Victorian lady in the garden. As Kincaid herself becomes the gardener, this entire set of associations is dismantled: not only because the British Garden is replaced by the mother's gardens,[44] but especially because that which is foregrounded of the practical act of gardening is the very impossibility of controlling nature, and that which is underlined by the title's subsumption of garden to the class 'book' is the further impossibility of separating nature from culture.[45] Thus the garden as metaphor gets a whole new life. This is deeply subversive, precisely because it is articulated by a prismatic voice which, although she refuses to speak as the subaltern and avoids being frozen into the language of the Other, nevertheless manages to bring the perspectives of a so-far silenced collectivity into the contemporary cultural debate; consequently and by necessity, she radically alters its epistemological frame. In *My Garden (Book):*, as well as in Kincaid's other texts, such collectivity expresses itself in standard English, rather than in Creole. The question of which language should be chosen by the colonized to make their voices heard is an open dilemma, which postcolonial writers have confronted in different manners. I personally doubt there is a universal, correct solution to this double-bind: Kincaid has chosen standard English perhaps because her narrators, as Merle Hodge pointedly observes, write fiction as if it were an essay and a realistic rendering of the speech of the collectivity would be a contrast with such rhetorical choice.[46] In *My Brother*, expressions in patois are confined within parentheses in the text, a choice which Sarah Brophy interprets as indicative not only of Kincaid's presentation of Devon both as a closeted homosexual whose speech hides under the protection of prophylactic parenthesis (meant to protect narrator and readers from his pathogenic power) and as a powerless colonialized subject whose language is indicative of his inferiority, but also of her refusal to speak for Devon.[47] Thus, she may choose standard over Creole English, as I imply above, because of her political refusal to speak as a subaltern and to treat the subaltern as a native informant. And yet, it might indeed be because of her presumed poor command of Creole, which in any case I would not equate to a betrayal of Caribbean culture.[48] What matters to me most is that her language, so deceptively simple and standard, produces such fundamental transformations in our parameters of interpretation that it manages to dismantle the ethnic versus Euroamerican opposition while never surrendering to silencing the colonized versus colonizer hierarchical relationship. One important transformation it forces upon our cognitive structure is the deconstruction of the all too frequent use of 'culture' as a totalizing explanation of 'difference.' Kincaid rather works on connections and networks, and even though she rightly retains a sense of place, she conceives of cultures as a travelling concept directed at fostering interaction and creating spaces.

The Second Chapter, 'Birthing Oneself: Identity On the Run,' is meant to emphasize that Kincaid's epistemological frame does not separate, as it were, Life 'right here' from Birth 'down there' and Death 'over there'. This traditional, modern, spatialized opposition between

Life and Death is rather overcome when she writes about Living as the experience of continuous becoming and passing through space and time and passing for a contextualized identity, and when her discourse includes birth and death, as the continuous birthing of oneself and as dying which is an inevitable part of living. That's why her subjectivities are always constructed as prisms — as multi-faceted entities which receive and give, which interact and relate to who and what passes through and is passed through by them and which can in turn pass for one or another color in different places.[49] These subjects are not simply given birth — they are continuously birthing themselves, engaging living as agents in terms which two prominent Caribbean poet-thinkers such as Audre Lorde and Lorna Goodison have so incisively proposed.[50] Their identities are always 'on the run,' as the Filipino-American performing artist Jessica Hagedorn puts it when describing her own 'definitionless' I.[51]

Finally, the Third Chapter, 'Living and Dying: the Other as Subject,' concentrates precisely on the confrontation of prismatic subjectivity with the inevitability of death. In her own terms, Jamaica Kincaid shares Edouard Glissant's and Wilson Harris's urge for a modern conceptualization of the sacred, the myth, and the epic. Observing that classical myth 'contains a hidden violence that catches in the links of filiation and absolutely challenges the existence of the other as an element of relation and that the Epic ... singles out a community in relation to the Other, and senses Being only as in-itself, because it never conceives of it as a relation,' Glissant calls for a modern epic capable of expressing 'political consciousness ... disengaged from civic frenzy and of ground(ing) lyricism in a confluence of speech and writing where things of the community, without being diminished (and without turning truths into generalities as Christian tragedy, as the work of Eliot or Claudel meant to do), would be the initiation to totality without renouncing the particular.'[52] Kincaid's narrative redefines myth and epic along these lines, in a way that has been explained by the writings of both Angela Carter and Derek Walcott, whose interest is more in the articulation of the contradictions inherent in the material world rather than in the metaphysical value of the inexplicable aspects of life. Unquestionably, she fully participates in the construction of 'the dialectic of totality,' which turns out to be 'driven by the thought of errantry.'[53] Indeed, for Kincaid, 'the thought of errantry' is a poetics, which always infers that at some moment it is told. The tale of errantry is 'the tale of Relation.'[54] Even though Kincaid does not avail herself of the Creole language, it seems clear to me that her narrative expresses that particular 'Relation' which Glissant attributes to be proper to the Creole language: 'Relation ... is not merely an encounter; a shock ... a *metissage*, but a new and original dimension allowing each person to be there and elsewhere, rooted and open, lost in the mountains and free beneath the sea, in harmony and in errantry.'[55]

If today it is both desirable that no single model of development is pursued and that no single nation should withdraw into its own secluded particularity, then Kincaid's non-totalizing and yet potentially universal voice points the way towards Glissant's 'totality' that has no need to be realized — a totality that is prismatic and relational like the subjects that inhabit it, an agency that is not only capable of transforming the world she inhabits but also of presenting herself as an ever-changing subjectivity. Her empowerment comes also from a thorough confrontation with the absence/nothingness which constitutes her own origin and the discriminations she has suffered with her impossible and yet necessary dream of love for a collectivity of humans capable of sharing a world globalized through the principles of ecological justice.[56]

Notes

1   Gayatri C. Spivak, *Outside in the Teaching Machine*, New York: Routledge, 1993, p. 171.

2   The phrase echoes Marie Cardinal, *Les Mots pour le dire*, Paris: Grasset & Fasquelle, 1975.

3   William V. Spanos uses the phrase 'rethinking thinking' in *America's Shadow*, Minneapolis: Minnesota UP, 2000, which provides a further forceful instance of his postmodernist theoretical critique. His perspective shares with the feminist theory I privilege the effort to modify the epistemological frame within which we cast our alternative visions. Since his path-breaking direction of the journal *boundary2*, Spanos has well represented what I refer to as a 'postmodernism of resistance,' as witnessed by the publication of Chandra T. Mohanty, 'Under Western Eyes: Feminist Scholarship and Colonial Discourses' in *boundary2*, 12/3 (Spring/ Fall 1984). I elaborate this position, on which the present study often relies, in Giovanna Covi, 'Decolonialized Feminist Subjects' in *Critical Studies on the Feminist Subject*, Trento: Dipartimento di Scienze Filologiche e Storiche, 1998: 19-56.

4   Stephanie Black, director and Jamaica Kincaid, script writer, *Life and Debt*, Tuff Gong Pictures, 2001.

5   Gayatri C. Spivak, 'Can the Subaltern Speak?' in Larry Grossberg and Cary Nelson, eds. *Marxism and the Interpretation of Culture*, Urbana: U of Illinois P, 1988: 271-313, thoroughly articulates the implicit question of my reasoning in this passage.

6   See Giovanna Covi, 'Decolonialized Feminist Subjects.'

7   Throughout, all references to Jamaica Kincaid's works are given parenthetically in the text.

8   See Adrienne Rich, *Of Woman Born: Motherhood as Experience and Institution*, New York: Norton, 1976, and *What is Found There, Notebooks on Poetry and Politics*, New York: Norton, 1993.

9   See Julia Kristeva, 'Women's Time' in *Signs* 7 (1981): 13-35.

10   Elaine Scarry, *On Beauty and Being Just*, Princeton: Princeton UP; 1999, p. 109.

11   Rosi Braidotti, *Metamorphoses: Towards a Materialist Theory of Becoming*, Cambridge: Polity Press, 2002.

12   See Eve K. Sedgwick, *Epistemology of the Closet*, Berkeley, CA: University of California Press, 1990.

13   See Martin Heidegger, (*Sein und Zeit*, Berlin 1926), *Being and Time*, New York Harper and Row, 1962.

14   See Gayatri C. Spivak, *Outside in the Teaching Machine*.

15   See Rosi Braidotti, *Nomadic Subject: Embodiment and Sexual Difference in Contemporary Feminist Theory*, New York: Columbia University Press, 1994.

16   For a pointed articulation of this difference, see Caren Kaplan, *Questions of Travel*, Durham: Duke University Press, 1996, p. 7.

17   Jamaica Kincaid and Eric Fischl, *Annie, Gwen, Lilly, Pam and Tulip*, (New York: Library Fellows of the Whitney Museum of Modern Art, 1986, limited edition) New York: Alfred A. Knopf, in association with the Whitney Museum, 1989. Moira Ferguson, to my knowledge, is the only critic who has given the deserved attention to this artwork; see Moira Ferguson, *Jamaica Kincaid: Where the Land Meets the Body*, U of Virginia P, 1994: 35-40. The five voices are experiencing the passing of childhood innocence and union with the world and foresee themselves as facing conflict in different manners; in the process, Ferguson sharply points out, 'they understand not only the importance of naming but the fact that naming in and of itself is not a tidy solution ... their voices redolent of life, announcing perpetual action and counteraction' (p. 40). This beautiful work of art already shows that the young narrator in *At the Bottom of the River* is aware of what she will encounter in *Annie John, Lucy* and *The Autobiography of My Mother* and qualifies her as being inclined towards a critical and complex understanding of her possibility to act upon the conflictual world expecting her entry.

18   Judith Butler would say 'a performance'; see both her *Gender Trouble: Feminism and the Subversion of Identity*, London: Routledge, 1990, and *Bodies that Matter: On the Discursive Limits of 'Sex'*, London: Routledge, 1993.

19   See Linda Alcoff, 'Cultural Feminism versus Poststructuralism: The Identity Crisis in Feminist Theory' in *Signs* 13 (Spring 1988): 405-36.

20   See Teresa de Lauretis, *Technologies of Gender: Essays on Theory, Film and Fiction*, Bloomington: Indiana University Press, 1986.

21   Gayatri C. Spivak, *In Other Worlds: Essays in Cultural Politics*, New York: Methuen, 1987.

22   Trinh Minh-ha T., *Woman/Native/Other: Writing Postcoloniality and Feminism*, Bloomington: Indiana University Press, 1989.

23 The most relevant of Kathy Acker's texts here are *Kathy Goes to Haiti*, Toronto: Rumor Publications, 1978 and *In Memoriam to Identity*, New York: Grove, 1990.

24 See Alice Walker, *In Search of Our Mother's Gardens*, New York: Harvest Books, 1983; and Audre Lorde, 'Poetry is Not a Luxury' in *Sister Outsider*, Traumansburg, NY: Crossing, 1984, p. 37.

25 For this articulation of sexual difference and gender I refer again to my essay 'Decolonialized Feminist Subjects,' which is indebted to, among others, Judith Butler's *Gender Trouble*, published in the same year as Kincaid's *Lucy*.

26 The term 'decolonialize' which I have elaborated to develop my own articulation of sexual difference and gender in 'Decolonialized Feminist Subjects' with the purpose of emphasizing the cultural revolution that must always join the liberation struggle, is borrowed from Angela Carter, 'Notes from the Frontline,' in Michelène Wandor, ed., *On Gender and Writing*, London: Pandora, 1983: 69-77.

27 Gayatri C. Spivak, *Outside in the Teaching Machine*, p. 78.

28 Gayatri C. Spivak, *Outside in the Teaching Machine*, p. 64.

29 Gayatri C. Spivak, *Outside in the Teaching Machine*, p. x.

30 See Caren Kaplan, *Questions of Travel*, for a theoretical elaboration of this point.

31 Gayatri C. Spivak, 'The Politics of Translation' in Michèle Barret and Anne Phillips, eds., *Destabilizing Theory: Contemporary Feminist Debates*, Palo Alto, CA: Stanford University Press, 1992:177-200, p. 192. In this paragraph I weave Spivak's concept of cultural translation together with the concept of passing referred to feminist subjectivity as elaborated by Liana Borghi, 'Introduzione: L'occhio del[l]'ago' in *Passaggi: Letterature comparate al femminile*, Urbino: Quattroventi, 2002. Throughout, I use the term 'passing' in Borghi's complex articulation.

32 Angela Carter, 'Notes from the Frontline,' p. 75.

33 See Lennard Davis, *Factual Fictions: The Origins of the English Novel*, Philadelphia: University of Pennsylvania Press, 1983.

34 Toni Morrison, 'The Site of Memory' (1987) in William K. Zinsser, ed. *Inventing the Truth: The Art and Craft of Memoir*, New York: Houghton Mifflin, 1995: 84-95, p. 90. and pp. 90-1. Zinsser's apt title, *Inventing the Truth*, clearly indicates the function of invention in this context.

35 The term is borrowed form Toni Morrison, *Beloved*, New York: Knopf, 1987 and theoretically presented in *Playing in the Dark*, New York: Vintage, 1992.

36 Wilson Harris, 'Quetzalcoatl and the Smoking Mirror (Reflections on Originality and Tradition)' (Address to Temenos Academy, London, 7 February 1994), *Review of Contemporary Fiction*, 17:2 (Summer 1997): 12-23.

37 Wilson Harris, 'Cross-Cultural Crisis: Imagery, Language and the Intuitive Imagination,' in *Commonwealth Lectures* (University of Cambridge), n. 2, Oct. 31, 1990.

38 Rikki Ducornet, *The Monstrous and the Marvelous*, San Francisco: City Lights, 1999, p. 116.

39 In the title of Chapter Two, I adapt the lines 'I / definitionless / a nervous running creature' from Jessica Hagedorn's poem 'Crimson Prey for Audre Lorde' in *Terra Nova*, Washington, 1989, to charge the phrase 'identity on the run' with the

meaning of identity-less identity; here I conjugate Hagedorn's 'on the run' with Liana Borghi's concept of 'passing.'

40   In this sense, my reading of Kincaid's works as a whole departs from Antonia MacDonald-Smythe's otherwise mostly shared perspective articulated in *Making Homes in the West/Indies: Construction of Subjectivity in the Writings of Michelle Cliff and Jamaica Kincaid*, New York: Garland, 2001. While she maintains that neither the mother nor her community ever change in Kincaid's narratives, thus reflecting a 'static' vision 'performed largely through the distance of memory' (p. 180), on the contrary I would emphasize Kincaid's capacity to revise, by repeating with a difference, her story of herself, her mother and her mother country. The reason why I do not see the 'ever-present danger that Kincaid's prolonged fascination with the 'I'/eye will create solipsistic, self-indulgent narratives devoid of an interactive engagement with community' (p. 188) lies in the fact that I do not see Kincaid 'construct[ing] through language 'the 'West Indian space in which [she] has made herself' (p. 189). The subjectivity I read in Kincaid's narratives, rather than constructed through language, is historically and materially grounded in the social reality that has shaped her initially and from which she always begins in order to redefine herself in different, distant and ever-changing contexts. As her voice moves from youth into maturity, moreover, a sense of belonging to a community is sharpened and contributes to making her subjectivity more relational and less oppositional.

41   See also Gayatri C. Spivak, *A Critique of Postcolonial Reason: Towards a History of the Vanishing Present*, Cambridge: Harvard Univ ersity Press, 1999, p. 388.

42   See Gayatri C. Spivak, 'Three Women Texts and a Critique of Imperialism' in Henry L. Gates, Jr., ed., *Race, Writing and Difference*, Chicago: University of Chicago Press, 1986: 262-80.

43   See Monika Fludernik, Donald Freeman, and Margaret Freeman, 'Metaphor and Beyond: An Introduction' *Poetics Today* 20:3 (Fall 1999): 383-96.

44   Alice Walker's 'gardens' can be contrasted here with the traditional figuration of the English Garden as successful example of domesticated nature and perfect home for the English Lady.

45   Donna Haraway, *Simians, Cyborgs and Women: the Reinvention of Nature*, New York: Routledge 1991, marks a turning point in feminist thinking with regard to the conceptualization of nature and culture. Adopting Haraway's cultural understanding of nature and the impossibility of distinguishing the two, I would dissociate from Susie O'Brien's ecocritical reading of Kincaid's *My Garden (Book)*: as an instance of a multicultural and environmentalist perspective in which hybridity expresses 'the heterogeneity between and within nature(s) and culture(s)' (p. 181), since 'nature and culture strive together without ever achieving total reconciliation' (p. 182). See Susie O'Brien, 'The Garden and the World: Jamaica Kincaid and the Cultural Borders of Ecocriticism' in *Mosaic* 35/2 (June 2002): 167-182.

46   Merle Hodge, 'Caribbean Writers and Caribbean Language: A Study of Jamaica Kincaid's *Annie John*' in *Winds of Change: The Transforming Voices*, Linda Strong-Leek, ed., New York: Peter Lang, 1998: 47-53, p. 53.

47   Sarah Brophy, 'Angels in Antigua: The Diasporic of Melancholy in Jamaica Kincaid's *My Brother*' in *PMLA* (March 2002): 265-77.

48   Some critics have argued this, a line I am not interested in pursuing. More interesting to me is Merle Hodge's claim that Kincaid avoids vernacular strategically, because class and cultural difference are not issues she wishes to thematize; see Merle Hodge, 'Caribbean Writers and Caribbean Language: A Study of Jamaica Kincaid's *Annie John*.' Rose-Myriam Réjouis, 'Caribbean Writers and Language' in *The Massachusetts Review*, 44:1/2 (Spring 2003),:213-232, interestingly argues that Kincaid genderizes the use of the vernacular by presenting it as unladylike, thus emphasizing the role of the mother as colonial educator, an interpretation also offered by Alison Donnell, 'When Daughters Defy' in *Women: A Cultural Review*, 4:1 (1993). Less convincingly, Isabel Hoving, *In Praise of New Travelers: Reading Caribbean Migrant Women's Writing*, Stanford, CA: Stanford University Press, 2001, speculates that the decision to keep patois at bay is compensated by the equally disturbing element of the mother's body as conveyor of anger (p. 221).

49   'Passing,' again, is used in the meaning articulated by Liana Borghi, 'Introduzione: L'occhio del[l]'ago.'

50   See Audre Lorde, 'Poetry is not a Luxury' and Lorna Goodison, *I Am Becoming My Mother*, London: New Beacon, 1986.

51   Jessica Hagedorn, 'Crimson Prey for Audre Lorde.'

52   Edouard Glissant, (*Le Discours Antillais*, 1981) *Caribbean Discourse*, Charlottesville: University Press of Virginia, 1989, p. 50 and p. 55.

53   Edouard Glissant, *Caribbean Discourse*, p. 17.

54   Edouard Glissant, *Caribbean Discourse*, p. 18.

55   Edouard Glissant, *Caribbean Discourse*, p. 34. The concept of 'errancy' brings me back to the 1980s and my first contacts with postmodernist theory, when William Spanos called my attention to the concept of 'errancy' in his reading of Herman Melville (see *The Errant Art of Moby Dick: The Cold War, The Canon, and the Struggle for American Literary Studies*, Durham: Duke UP, 1995). I like to recall my own intellectual meandering as a way to emphasize the importance of deconstructing instead of replacing previous interpretations of texts; like Kincaid who keeps retelling her own story, I think of criticism as an act of retracing my understanding: rather than being marked by a process which substituted a postmodernism of resistance with a focus on Caribbean identity, I would like for my feminist appreciation of Kincaid to show affiliations with as many approaches as are needed to account for the complexity of our own being in a relational world.

56   See Gayatri C. Spivak, *A Critique of Postcolonial Reason*, Chapter Four, on the necessity of dreaming the impossible world of ecological justice; in Chapter Three I expand on the relationship between Spivak's and Kincaid's articulations of this idea.

Chapter One

Epistemic Subversions in a Caribbean Voice: Jamaica Kincaid as a Lyrical Theorist

A Small Place — 'Ovando' — 'On Seeing England for the First Time' — My Garden (Book):

My reading of Kincaid's essayistic writings — a discourse which is 'thinking/poetry'[1] — aims to articulate the importance that her discourse plays transnationally as well as to focus on the most valuable theoretical framework for encouraging an expanded international feminist epistemological and political appreciation of her Caribbean-centred, thought-provoking, and lyrically beautiful narratives. Indeed, for too long, this US-based writer from Antigua has been read only as an African-American, or from the point of view of African-American criticism; only more recently, has Kincaid received critical attention as a Caribbean writer. My purpose is to show the extent to which her voice crosses national and cultural boundaries to articulate a discourse which addresses the global sphere while remaining historically grounded in its local specificity. I wish to attempt a 'glocal' appreciation of her discourse in the effort to account for its profound complexity. Without ever pretending to be universal, this discourse is shareable by feminists across cultures: it moves beyond identity politics to indicate a cultural program for the collectivity. It also resists any attempt to reduce prismatic identity solely to nation, race or gender; rather, it successfully accounts for contemporary networking power relations by proposing fractal figurations of subjectivity and contexts.[2] In Caren Kaplan's terms, I argue that Kincaid's work convincingly shows how the figure of the exile and the dichotomy centre-periphery serve to support the western ideology of democracy as assimilation and of nation as naturalization;[3] it launches a devastating critique against the romanticization of the metropolitan experience in order to privilege those transnational circuits of capital and power that have determined cultural production in the Caribbean. The essays included in this chapter take us from explorations and colonial exploitation to postcolonial domination and global imperialism by showing differences as well as similarities among the various forms of prevarication. For instance, terms such as exploration, discovery, and exploitation are linked both to the colonists' arrival in the Americas in 'Ovando' and to the botanists' voyage through China in *My Garden (Book):*. In addition, tracing Kincaid's evaluation of colonialism through these texts underlines the consistency with which her writing never lends itself to being subsumed under a romanticized conception of diaspora as cosmopolitan exilic and hybrid condition: in her discourse, subjectivities are clearly always influenced by economic forces of migration as well as by cultural process of identification and self-definition.

In these essays, Kincaid's prismatic identity casts a gaze on its own colonial past and into its own relational existence, and then aims not at an ideal goal in the future but rather at a declaredly unattainable albeit necessary collective dream whose purpose is boosting the prism's cognitive elaboration and pragmatic agency within society. It fully accepts the challenge to identity-building by looking into the mystery of who it is rather than resting on a given definition of what it is, thus tackling the question of coming to terms with history from a theoretical point of view and explicitly redefining history as discourse. Within this framework, I find that Spivak's concept of 'cultural translation' well expresses Kincaid's theory/practice of the writing of subjectivities conceived as passing entities, which circulate in different contexts and are never frozen into the transcendental icon of a single identity. Her writing works in the silent spaces between and around words; it expresses 'things for which no language previously existed,' thus creating the 'condition and effect of knowing,' which 'allows the world to be made of an agent who acts in it in an ethical, a political, a day-to-day way.'[4] It is exactly as cultural translations that I read Kincaid's essays. Like translations, they take up the impossible challenge of finding words which did not exist before and, again like translations, they are temporary words, which follow previous utterances and will be followed by further attempts to articulate the yet unsaid.

This perspective enables me to focus on what I deem her main concern, that is, the articulation of the effects of colonialism on subjectivity, specifically on female subjectivity, and on postcolonial agency. It also allows me to account for the strict relation between issues of socio-historical power and her definition of sexualized subjectivity. Kincaid's essays pursue their ideas with passionate stubbornness, which gives an impressive 'backbone' to the writings I am discussing in this chapter. My critical decision to place her essays in the foreground of her fiction calls attention to the equally foregrounded interrelationship in Kincaid's writing between the discourse of colonialism — and by implication of race and class — and the discourse of patriarchy. Her oeuvre passionately and stubbornly hammers the idea that subjectivity emerges when ideologically pre-constituted identities, on the basis of such parameters as gender, race, nationality and class, interrupt one another to confront their respective biases and enforce their various powers with reference to a specific political agenda capable of accounting for the complexity of our being in the world.

Not least, the organization of my analysis also aims at underlining my own critical effort to avoid subordinating Kincaid's theory/poetry to theoretical discourse. In its diversity and nevertheless by virtue of its inescapable social implications, her lyrical voice runs parallel with research and expression more explicitly integrated in a process of liberation which moves beyond national independence to foresee a global context which is more and more decentred and in which it is possible to theorize and practice an alterity/subjectivity without risking appropriation and exclusion. Her theorizing is strictly linked to her risk-taking empirical work as a writer and thus reaches the strategic effect Spivak invokes when she disclaims 'theories of essences.'[5] Indeed, the essays I have grouped in this first chapter are inextricably linked to the (auto)biographical fictional narratives of the following chapters: their discourse is equally articulated by a prismatic subjectivity that is always contextualized and struggling to relate to others whom she also regards as prismatic.

A Small Place (1988)[6]

'If you go to Antigua as a tourist' are the first words of A Small Place, the purpose of which is to explain the intricate situation of colonial history and postcolonial exploitation of Kincaid's native country to a European and American audience. Its slim 80 pages are divided into four parts, each of which is a critical reflection on the socio-political reality of Antigua considered from a different angle. One of the Leeward Islands in the West Indies, it became an independent state, along with two smaller islands, in 1981. Elaine Cynthia Potter Richardson (Jamaica Kincaid) was born in this British colony in 1949, of a mother and father who gave her African, Carib Indian, and Scottish racial identity, making her a true American, in the sense assigned by Jack Forbes to the term.[7] She left Antigua at seventeen to become an au pair in Scarsdale, New York, and despite the fact that she has lived in the United States all these years, she has never renounced her Antiguan citizenship. Moira Ferguson pointedly observes that the conditional that opens *A Small Place* — 'If you go' — ironically stresses the fact that there are not tourists who would ask all the fundamental political questions hypothesized in the essay; on the contrary, the common mindless type of travellers 'are 'ugly' human beings who are indulging in hollow pleasures' and thus are, like the colonizers, 'morally culpable' of racism and exploitation of the Third and Fourth Worlds.[8] However, I think the text develops an even more intricate complexity than this clear-cut condemnation indicates.

A Small Place poses a problem of genre definition[9] common in various ways to all of Kincaid's writing. In her two previous works of poetic fiction — *At the Bottom of the River* and *Annie John* — the charm comes primarily from shifting the reader's perspective between autobiography and novel, between collection and series of short stories, in a continuous mixture of dream and reality that disrupts the assumption that fact and fiction stand separated. This rocking-chair effect is obtained through a repetitive, child-like language whose lexicon and syntax are of the utmost simplicity. *A Small Place* is a political essay in content, but it reads like fiction, while sounding like a speech delivered with the passion and rhythm of a song; the result is that of a lyrical, powerful essay whose beauty is only matched by Cynthia Krupat's drawings. The general effect is that of a pageant told by a ballad-singer, and this is definitely a new rhetorical way of delivering theoretical thinking.

This philosophical song manages to express the most elaborate analysis of a complex and intricate political situation, exactly in the same way as the dream-like perspective of the girl, narrator and protagonist of her previous works, provides a sophisticated and non-dogmatic feminist definition of the postcolonial subjectivity of an African-Caribbean woman. While constantly complaining about the inadequacy of words, Kincaid in all her books succeeds in articulating the contradictions and ambiguities of postcolonialism and global power, rendering in sparkling images the paradoxical and scandalous condition of a well-defined historical place.

This is possible because her use of language is deceptively simple. The transparency of the elaborate political message betrays a faked primitive, child-like voice and the reader soon realizes that the text functions at multiple levels and the tableaux are indeed multi-layered palimpsests. Under the pretended naiveté of the speaking-voice lies a deeper connotative significance generated by lexical repetitions whose rhythmic effect is counterpointed by the sharp political satire of the authorial voice, which fluctuates between foreground and background. The artless simplicity of the syntax is also delusive: right at the beginning, a few basic clauses are tailgated by an elaborate narrative expanding over a two-page long sentence, a construction that no child could possibly master with such balance and stylistic accuracy. The sentences are often chained to add momentum and emphasis to the message, like in the opening twelve-page paragraph of the third part in which the authoritative narrative voice expresses her 'bitterness' and 'shame' (SP 41) at the present state of her island.

Each part is organized around a repetition of sound and lexical patterns slightly but significantly dissimilar, as if the ballad-singer had to address four different audiences from four different perspectives. It is analogous to a jazz composition played on various instruments — always the same theme — but developed in multiple voices and variations. The narrator sometimes repeats and even contradicts herself; at other points, she switches back and forth and in so doing turns sameness into difference and vice versa, in an endless movement that refuses to chain her to either a single voice or a fixed point of view. Significantly, the result is not that of a heterogeneous indifferent fluidity; rather, it produces a message that sustains its temporality throughout the essay. Thanks to the precise historicization of the context, difference here always makes a difference. The protest voice is enriched by a chorus that contextualizes and relativizes her rage, thus politicizing a reaction which is never allowed to withdraw into a psychological confinement.[10] The sound and word repetitions express the struggle against ideology and dogma, in a way that is no less powerful than the opposition to injustice and racism expressed by the logical organization of the discourse. Form and content constantly comment on each other, preventing the petrifaction of thought.

Furthermore, each part is organized according to parallel shifts in voice and focus. Reading *A Small Place* is like looking at the sea: the message is carried by the tide, but it is impossible to say upon which particular wave. It is indeed a polyphonic work whose sounds cannot be isolated and whose voices cannot be separated, and yet they can be identified, because their identity is relational, prismatic. The narrator slides in and out of the events of the story, continuously adopting the perspective of different constituencies.

In the first part, a song-like outpouring voices the narrator's relentless, sarcastic disapproval of the obtuse tourist in Antigua. Ferguson states that 'Kincaid's condemnation is absolute and unsparing' and that in this first part she treats tourists 'no better than slave owners.'[11] Treated with mocking irony and addressed directly as 'you,' the hapless foreigner becomes the focus of the first description of the island. Therefore, this is presented intra-diegetically through the narrow and ridiculous point of view:

> An ugly thing, that is what you are when you become a tourist, an ugly, empty thing, a stupid thing, a piece of rubbish pausing here and there to gaze at this and taste that, and it will never occur to you that the people who inhabit the place in which you have just paused cannot stand you, that behind their closed doors they laugh at your strangeness (you do not look the way they look); the physical sight of you does not please them; you have bad manners (it is their custom to eat their food with their hands; you try eating their way, you look silly; you try eating the way you always eat, you look silly); they do not like the way you speak (you have an accent); they collapse helpless from laughter, mimicking the way they imagine you must look as you carry out some everyday bodily function. They do not like you. (*SP* 17)

The gaze is that of a person who is incapable of thinking. However, by rhetorically pointing out what the tourist misses, the narrator integrates an otherwise limited and biased picture. There is no danger of a narrow perspective: the point of view and mode of narration is constantly expanded and stretched to include opposite and diverse foci, as the last sentence in the above passage illustrates.

'They do not like you' anticipates the shift that concludes Part One- a paragraph that turns the perspective to the natives (*SP* 18-19). Just like the tourist who 'ordinarily' is 'a nice person' (*SP* 15), they are not unblemished heroes. They both suffer from a life of 'banality and boredom and desperation and depression,' the difference being that the tourist can escape it, while the natives are 'too poor' to do so (*SP* 18-19). This reversed focus serves a double function: it dismantles the binary opposition tourist/native and connects the First to the Second Part.

Here the narrator concentrates on her own past, a history of slavery and colonization which she tells again in a double voice. The first is the candid eye of the colonized girl she was, the second the outraged opinion of the author she has become, a person full of indignation for having been forced 'to see the world through England' (*SP* 33). The English filter seems as blinding for the native protagonist as the tropical sun is for the tourist and Antiguans are depicted as being exemplary of mimicking; Ferguson observes that Kincaid implies that 'Vec Bird perpetuates British colonialism in a different way.'[12] It takes the intervention of the extradiegetic voice of the authoritative narrator to explicate what the girl calls the 'bad manners' of the various colonizers: 'No one ever dreamed that the word for any of this was racism' (*SP* 27, 29). This line invites the reader to translate the term 'ill-mannered' with 'racist' each time it appears in the previous pages:[13] now we understand that it applies to the English as well as to the Americans, and even to those Europeans who have themselves suffered discrimination, like the Czech doctor who fled from Hitler and the Northern Irish headmistress, who should certainly know about British colonialism. A passage like this reflects San Juan's call for a 'socially oriented semiotics . . . committed to the elimination of the hegemonic discourse of race' and cannot be silenced nor subsumed under the generic label of 'post-colonial discourse.'[14] This is a voice which uncompromisingly moves through poetry to stretch and reach the actual political fight for those cultures inhabiting the cutting edge of survival. In Ferguson's terms, *A Small Place* is 'counterknowledge with a vengeance.'[15]

Therefore a contrapuntal structure transmits the contradictions and injustices undergone by a colonized, enslaved people. Three pages before the ending, two narrative voices — one external and one internal to the events — merge in a fugal stretto passage in which a focal reversal turns again on the intradiegetic addressee. The 'you' has become a 'master' and is blamed for post-colonial corruption derived from the imposition of the 'English' view of the world:

But then again, perhaps as you observe the debacle in which I now exist, the utter ruin that I say is my life, perhaps you are remembering that you had always felt people like me cannot run things. . . . (*SP* 36)

And a few lines later we find the explanation:

Do you know why people like me are shy about being capitalists? Well, it's because we, for as long as we have known you, were capital, like bales of cotton and sacks of sugar, and you were the commanding cruel capitalists, and the memory of this is so strong, the experience so recent, that we can't quite bring ourselves to embrace this idea that you think so much of. (*SP* 36-7)

A cutting statement then concludes this analysis:

Even if I really came from people who were living like monkeys in trees, it was better to be that than what happened to me, what I became after I met you. (*SP* 37)

This outburst of anger leads nicely into Part Three, which opens with a speaking-I focusing on herself and her addressee. The native invites her white interlocutor to imagine how she feels when telling about the corruption of the post-colonial Antiguan government; this is how, in the longest section of the essay, 'rage' becomes 'bitterness and shame' (*SP* 41). But only one-third of the way through this section, the intra-homodiegetic narrator leaves room for an impersonal external voice recounting what 'the people in a small place' do (*SP* 51). In the narrative tide, this is no distinct wave either: the autobiographical voice soon intrudes (*SP* 57) to cast a judgment on the people of the island, in what is a complete reversal of the roles assigned to intra- and extra-diegetic voices in the First Part. This time, in fact, it is the speaking-I who shows more knowledge than the omniscient narrator wondering who her people are. She concludes that they must be 'a combination' of 'children,' 'artists' and 'lunatics,' and then lets them speak for ten pages, 'in a voice that suggests all three' (*SP* 57). This tri-tonal voice lists some of the major scandals in Antigua: drug dealing and its connection to offshore banks; members of the government engaging in such business as importing Japanese cars (the main market being the government itself), prostitution and gambling; government corruption such as 'electric and telephone poles' also carrying 'the heavier wiring for cable television' at public expense (*SP* 58), special ammunition being tested in Antigua to be shipped to the government of South Africa (*SP* 61), or meat 'contaminated by radiation' distributed in Antigua (*SP* 61); political crime committed by Syrian and Lebanese real estate owners as well as by the US Army based on the island (*SP* 63); robberies, like the disappearance of French developmental aid funds (*SP* 66); and finally the fact that the country's ministers are legal residents of the US (*SP* 68). Facts are named, and it is this practice of naming which renders Kincaid's discourse a political engagement in the decolonization not only of the nation-state but also of its culture and people, rather than a mere contribution to the all-encompassing academic debate on 'post-coloniality.' In fact, the list of the scandals in the newly independent state of Antigua brings us directly from the British old empire to the US new empire, and *A Small Place* moves rapidly from the articulation of slavery and colonialism to the discourse of the imperialism of American hegemony and the domination of multinational capital.

Pointed, serious, and specific as these accusations may sound, they do not seem effective enough to the impersonal voice who intrudes twice to spin out the political implications of this state of affairs. Of the two parenthetical statements — one concerns banks and the other gambling — the first cannot be overlooked. Here the narrator ironically points out the relationship between Swiss neutrality and Antiguan corruption:

> . . . not a day goes by that I don't hear of some criminal kingpin, some investor, who has a secret Swiss bank account. But maybe there is no connection between the wonderful life the Swiss lead and the ill-gotten money that is resting in Swiss bank vaults; maybe it's just a coincidence. (*SP* 60)

International political and economic connections are spelled out very clearly and the philosophy supporting them is not understated either. Here is what follows the quotation above:

> The Swiss are famous for their banking system and for making superior timepieces. Switzerland is a neutral country, money is a neutral commodity, and time is neutral, too, being neither here nor there, one thing or another. (*SP* 60)

The complicity of a linear concept of time in the violent mastering of the world is underlined not only by a sustained, non-logocentric development of the story, but also by continuous references to the cultural meaning of a Euro-centric, metaphysical structure of consciousness. In these parts, the essay insists on the importance of re-membering, discovering the radical temporality of Being that a spatial, metaphysical orientation has domesticated and silenced in its effort to master existence. But what makes Kincaid's discourse more convincingly and genuinely political than most philosophical debates is her anchoring these observations to a historically defined situation. We are made aware of the fact that the 'small place' in the following apparently universal statement is Antigua: 'To the people in a small place, the division of Time into the Past, the Present, and the Future does not exist' (*SP* 54). The political implications of the spatialization of time are pointed out already in Part One, when — with reference to the library constantly under repair — the ironic voice assuming the thoughts of the tourist comments: 'you might see this as a sort of quaintness on the part of these islanders, these people descended from slaves — what a strange, unusual perception of time they have' (*SP* 9). The issue is too fundamental to be hinted at only in passing, and in the next page the narrator spells out how 'the West got rich' by exploiting the people and resources of the Third World: 'what a great part the invention of the wristwatch played in it, for there was nothing noble-minded men could not do when they discovered they could slap time on their wrists just like that' (*SP* 10).

Therefore, in one of the most important topics discussed in *A Small Place*, Kincaid provides an instance of a temporal treatment both of structure and of theme: historical — as opposed to mythical — repetition characterizes the entire discourse; memory interacts with the present, rather than freezing into a nostalgic paralysis; the recurring pattern is not a litany, but a way of showing connections on a larger and larger scale. Repetition opens up the discourse to new possibilities, like at the end of the tale by three Antiguan voices, who explain their need for expansion in these terms:

> And it is in that strange voice, then — the voice that suggests innocence, art, lunacy — that they say these things, pausing to take breath before this monument to rottenness, that monument to rottenness, as if they were tour guides; as if, having observed the event of tourism, they

have absorbed it so completely that they have made the degradation and humiliation of their daily lives into their own tourist attraction. (*SP* 69)

And yet, one more time we shouldn't believe that the new voice is superior to the previous one, nor that it proposes to replace it. The structure of this essay is dialogic, yet the discourse it produces is profoundly respectful of inerasable differences produced by historical discrimination within the dialogue: the narrative is resumed by the impersonal narrator to attack the national as well as the international scene and to establish connections between Antigua's depression, the US invasion of Grenada and the Baby Doc scandal in Haiti; nevertheless, the comparative political analysis is reported as the making of those same natives that in the quotation above have been scolded for their political passivity. It is 'them' who 'anchor' (*SP* 69-74) the events together and see what sort of dictatorship their independent government has turned into, a dictatorship likely to face 'death, only this time at the hands of the Americans' (*SP* 74).

This naturally leads to the omniscient narrator of the last section in which paradox and opposites are accepted and in which the 'you' and the 'I' blur into a mutual 'human beings' (*SP* 81). The distance of the narrative voice makes this last turn in the story dream-like, as if blurring the differences between masters and slaves were not only historically unacceptable but also romantically unattainable. This is why, more materialistically, the final utopian image is not for a world exceptionally united by love but more commonly for one populated by regular human beings. This is why the tone is more sombre and balanced; it describes the present situation of Antigua, declaring that there are no longer masters to be angry at and slaves to be proud of — rather, there is mostly average banality. The new situation is rendered through the oxymoronic repetition of descriptions of the beauties and miseries of the land (*SP* 78), a land that is both real and unreal and for that reason it is a prison of beauty. Indeed this is the best metaphor to describe the post-colonial condition: 'the unreal way in which it is beautiful now that they are free people is the unreal way in which it was beautiful when they were slaves' (*SP* 80). The 'prison of beauty' is the oxymoron of post-colonialism, a situation that is often one of a freedom received as a gift from the enemy, rather than won. Kincaid points this out:

> No Industrial Revolution, no revolution of any kind, no Age of Anything, no world wars, no decades of turbulence balanced by decades of calm. Nothing, then, natural or unnatural, to leave a mark on their character. (*SP* 79-80)

The conclusion serves as a logical explanation of the tidal movement of the whole essay:

> Of course, the whole thing is, once you cease to be a master, once you throw off your master's yoke, you are no longer human rubbish, you are just a human being, and all the things that add up to. So, too, with the slaves. Once they are no longer slaves, once they are free, they are no longer noble and exalted; they are just human beings. (*SP* 81)

And once our mode of thinking by a binary logic has ridded itself of the Hegelian dichotomy of Master and Slave, we are left with what Thomas Pynchon has called the 'bad shit' of the 'excluded middles' and a whole new world-picture to re-invent, tentative, fragmentary, relative but thankfully dynamic and dialogic and certainly historically grounded.[16] 'Kincaid conflates two sets of people ... then teases them apart,' observes Ferguson, and she manages to do so by articulating her usual representation of the mother-daughter relationship in a way that functions 'in dual chronologies, the colonial and the postcolonial.'[17]

Since the 1980's, Kincaid has engaged the creation of this new episteme, re-thinking mostly sexual and racial differences in *At the Bottom of the River*, *Annie John*, and *Lucy*, and relationships between the so-called Third World and Post-industrialized countries in *A Small Place*, 'On Seeing England for the First Time' and later in *My Garden (Book):*. In both cases, she has articulated the issues in terms other than those of a complementary opposition, by way of adopting a repetitive logic which adds, modifies, but never abrogates the previous positions. In her fictional works, she criticizes the very existence of sexual and racial difference, rather than the modes of their existence: her approach leaves no room for reform, invoking a radical change of structures, not simply of guards. The same is true for her first political essay: it moves far beyond the protest pamphlet, into a deep analysis and exploration of new frames for social and human comprehension.

The syntax, sounds and structure of the essay imitate this new process of understanding. Her inquiry requires logical thinking to move back and forth, in order to avoid the traps deriving from a reduction to a linear progression which would result in the glorification of slaves who no longer exist — or to a binary opposition — which could only interpret the corruption of the slaves-who-no-longer-exist in terms of the old masters. Repetitions and parallelisms enhance the importance of her circular and linear logic, an example of how the process of Deriddean repetition and trace can be put into practice and acquire political significance. Kincaid's voice provides a radical instance of a monumental, multi-levelled history. Here différance produces not only many differences, but enhances their possibility of making a significant difference in the distribution of power in the world.

In *A Small Place* repetition is never a repetition of the same. It is deeply grounded in the celebration of what Iris Murdoch has called the 'messiness' of existence: only the interaction between past and present, the memory of a reality governed by masters and slaves can fully comprehend a situation in which such a dichotomy has ceased to function. In its dismantling of the symmetrical, linear tale of the metaphysical interpretation of the world, Kincaid's book inevitably deviates from the literary canon. More importantly, it does so by clearly enhancing the inevitable significance of memory and history, therefore placing itself beyond — and not against or above — metaphysics. For Kincaid, her slave ancestors are there at the bottom of the Caribbean sea for us to remember, or rather, to re-memory, as Toni Morrison's *Beloved* has emphasized. In Antigua, the recollection of British colonialism becomes a Foucauldian counter-memory and it permits us to draw a connection between post-/neo-colonialism and post-capitalism, allowing a better understanding of international politics. This is why a ten-by-twelve-mile island becomes emblematic of the role imposed on the poorer countries of the world by the globalization of the financial and commercial markets.

The devastating effects of this neo-imperialist policy are loudly denounced in the video *Life and Debt* (2001) by Stephanie Black, which uses a script based on *A Small Place*. 'If you go to Jamaica as a tourist,' are the first and last words of this video containing numerous interviews to narrate the story of Jamaica's economy after independence. In clear-cut terms, the video deplores the IMF policy for serving only the interests of the most powerful countries of the world, headed by the US. Opening with the TV images of unrest in the streets of Kingston and the killing of young lives, the camera weaves contrasting pictures: on the one hand, social degradation, violence, exploited low-wage workers, emigrants, deluded farmers, Manley effectively explaining the unreasonable conditions imposed by the IMF upon his country and the tragic consequences that followed, and some Rastafarians and independent farmers who still militantly struggle for the survival of Jamaica's culture and social dignity; on the other hand, the camera focuses on mindless tourists disembarking in Montego Bay, an advertisement promoting ice-cream through the slogan 'one world 31 flavours', the IMF representative imperturbably spelling out his rules, containers loaded with US products inundating the Jamaican market and thwarting local farmers' initiatives. Through detailed stories explaining how the cultivation of bananas, onions, coffee, potatoes, lettuce, meat and dairy products dramatically declined when Jamaica was forced to abandon a policy for a self-sustaining economy, the video takes us to the sensational farce of the 'Free Zone' story. In this area, which has been declared not even a part of Jamaica, the Hanes factory produced underwear marketed as 'made in the USA': the official version, that Hanes was helping Jamaica pay its debt to the IMF, falls to pieces even in the eyes of its blinder supporters when Jamaicans see their working conditions dramatically reduced to new slavery and then their jobs handed over to imported Asian workers; finally, the factory closes business and leaves behind only its skeleton building. The interviewees make it clear that the IMF loans not only did not reduce poverty or produce growth, as even the official IMF report eventually admitted, but also destroyed the country's self-respect. Jamaica witnessed the passage from the Queen to MacDonald's to learn that 'life and debt' is 'freedom not yet,' as the sound track repeatedly reminds us.

What makes *A Small Place* adaptable to this recontextualization is not only its political stance, but also its insistence on an ontological philosophy, on a conception of human being as thrown into the midst of a worldly chaos, which casts a particular philosophical light on Kincaid's experimental treatment of the essay. Here is what a traditional 'objective' reporter of political facts would never say:

> an exact account, a complete account, of anything, anywhere, is not possible. (The hour in the day, the day of the year some ships set sail is a small, small detail in any picture, any story; but the picture itself, the story itself depend on things that can never, ever be pinned down.)

> The people in a small place can have no interest in the exact, or in completeness, for that would demand a careful weighing, careful consideration, careful judging, careful questioning. It would demand the invention of silence, inside of which these things could be done. (*SP* 53)

It represents an effort to say things from outside the tradition of the 'Age of Enlightenment,' which 'has done us very little good' (*SP* 36). The protest against a world that excludes and discriminates is uttered without, in turn, excluding and discriminating, that is, silencing other voices. Kincaid has indeed invented a silence in which all the Others, those excluded by the phallic and racist identity of the Western tradition, have found a voice, the voice of a Woman, of an Afro-American, of a Caribbean, of a radical militant, of a tender child, and possibly of many more that I don't recognize. What matters the most is that she has given these voices a way of neither speaking as mimics nor remaining silenced as subalterns: she has created a polyphonic sound which unites but never assimilates the various melodies. In this music, the One ('the human rubbish' that became the 'master') and the Other (the 'noble and exalted' people who became the slaves') are no longer polarized ('they are just human beings' *SP* 81), and a search for a critically postcolonial and a feminist/womanist positioning of the subject — instrumental for a radical engagement in the present historical conjuncture — is shown to be compatible with the rejection of a teleological picture of the world and the struggle to articulate a politics of relation, collectivity, and complex negotiations.

'Ovando' (1989)

'Ovando' might appear at first to parallel only the section of *A Small Place* in which slavery and colonialism are criticized as criminal acts, while the victims are declared to be 'noble and exalted.'[18] The story imagines slavery and colonialism to be personified by a zombie who comes to the door of the narrator's home wearing an armour, 'a complete skeleton except for his brain ... growing smaller by the millennium' ('O' 75) and who 'had made himself a body from plates of steel ... stained with shades of red, blood in various stages of decay' ('O' 75) — a monstrous body which becomes more and more hideous and, as the description of his deeds unfolds, grows 'an enormous tail' and 'horns on either side of his head' ('O' 80) until finally 'his head had taken the shape of a groundworm' ('O' 81).

However, things are not so clear-cut, even within the economy of this Gothic short-story told in the apparent style of a fanciful tale. On the one hand, we have the evil associated at the onset with the historical figure of Frey Nicolas de Ovando[19] and personified right away by the monstrous figure; on the other hand, we have the good represented by the first-person narrator who is identified clearly as one of Ovando's actual victims, a female Arawak or Carib Indian. The two figures are not predictably linked to two separate chains of positive and negative values. The fairy-tale atmosphere only enhances the documentary accuracy of the human horror and cultural devastation of that part of European history which took place in the Caribbean beginning in the sixteenth century, and the two modes together achieve a high level of complexity.

We are in Hispaniola, on the island which the Spanish called Santo Domingo and later colonialism divided into the Spanish Dominican Republic and French Haiti;[20] here in 1502 Frey Nicolas de Ovando became the first General Captain of the Indies (1502-1509) and founded *La Ciudad de Ovando*, Santo Domingo, enjoying the reputation of first urban developer of the New World and offering hospitality to Christopher Columbus during his fourth voyage. Frey Nicolas de Ovando earned another distinguishing element of his reputation: he was first to impose slavery upon the indigenous population causing their extermination and he began the importation of African slaves to Hispaniola after Bartolomé de las Casas's intervention with the Spanish Monarchy on behalf of the Taino population. His exploitation of the Africans brought no advantage to the natives, since Ovando is equally remembered for his brutal treatment of the Indios. Autobiographically, Kincaid's narrator represents both the Indios and the Africans exploited, murdered, and enslaved in the Americas: this should not be overlooked because the story places emphasis on the significance of her survival contrasted with the colonizer's figuration as a living dead since his first apparition. On the contrary, the Carib woman narrator is not only given the role of historian; she is also presented as a voice who is conscious of her physical as well as her intellectual identity, neither of which are granted to Ovando, who is reduced instead to a skeleton and an armour with a shrinking brain ('O' 75). The colonized-narrator's radical re-thinking of the history of Western colonialization, derives from a cognitive activity which is grounded both in the body and in the mind, thus rejecting a dichotomy upon which rests the culture of the Enlightenment that has sustained colonialism.

Kincaid's discourse represents an epistemological break and celebrates the survival of the enslaved people.

Indeed, this appears evident as soon as the colonized narrator introduces the colonizer: 'Immediately I was struck by his suffering ... Immediately I was struck by his innocence' ('O' 75). She foregrounds his 'suffering' and his 'innocence' and makes sure that the latter unambiguously refers to his being simple and lacking intellect only, and not to a naive and blameless trait in his character: 'Immediately I was struck by his innocence: for he had made himself a body from plates of steel ... and he thought I would not know the difference' ('O' 75). This introduction has the immediate effect of deconstructing not only the colonial expectation by which 'innocence' and 'suffering' belong to the presumed limited understanding of the natives, but also of imposing a subversive epistemological break upon the interpretation of the relationship between colonizer and colonized. The latter does not acquire a voice through liberation; rather, she has always possessed a voice whose cognitive superiority comes precisely from her awareness of the body, from her capacity to conjugate the mind with the body, and thus to see the difference between a body and an armour.

The colonized, the text emphasizes, never lost her voice; on the contrary, it is Ovando and his 'relatives in Spain, Portugal, France, England, Germany, Italy, Belgium, and the Netherlands' who 'lost the ability to speak and could only make pronouncements' ('O' 76). It is as if the Europeans, having acquired the ability to write, had lost touch with their oral culture, a culture which is carried by bodies, versus one which is stored in 'banks' ('O' 75). On the contrary, a dialogic interaction made of speaking and listening is clearly intended by the narrator when she raises the issue of her 'sympathy' and 'trust' ('O' 75). Ovando, in fact, having 'lost the ability to speak' can only devote himself to 'map-making' ('O' 77). And his realization that the world is round rather than flat is translated into the act of colonization: 'If the earth were round, thought Ovando, he could go away' ('O' 76). In so doing, Ovando 'carried a large piece of paper ... had rendered flat the imagined contents of his world. Oh what an ugly thing to see ... It looked like sadness itself, for it was a map. ... At that moment the world broke ('O' 76-77). 'Ovando sees the world as round because imperial ideology sees the world without frontiers ... round is a metaphor for marauding,' Ferguson pointedly remarks, while 'to be flat signif[ies] stability, a sense of community, of relating of belonging.'[21] By contrast, the colonized accepts the 'flatness' of the world and for her, as a consequence, 'all discovery results in contemplation' ('O' 78).

Exactly because colonizer and colonized have never stood in opposite relation to one another as humans but only as performers of their social roles, colonization and slavery comes as an act of magic, unexpectedly and surprisingly: "My Sheer Might!' said Ovando' ('O' 79) and 'in that moment, I, my world, and everything in it became Ovando's thralls' ('O' 80). Ovando transforms into a monstrous creature — 'his head had taken the shape of a groundworm' ('O' 81) — who destroys secular trees in order to produce paper on which to write 'that he dishonored [her]' ('O' 80).

The final charge against Ovando is an excess of egocentrism. If a Gothic story is the narration of a nightmare, then 'Ovando' has exhausted its narrative energy in representing the monster and cannot pursue the killing of the dragon. In fact, the narrator refuses to be the one who casts her judgment against Ovando, thus refusing to fall into the trap of the logic of colonialism by simply reversing it, and concludes:

> a charge against Ovando, then, is that he loved himself so that all other selves and all other things became nothing to him. ... And so it came to be that Ovando loved nothing, lived in nothing, and died just that way. I cannot judge Ovando. I have exhausted myself laying out before him his transgressions. I am exhausted from shielding myself so that his sins do not obsess and so possess me. ('O' 83)

Ovando is a traveller because he wants to possess and conquer. On the contrary, the narrator who refuses to possess and be possessed is a traveller in that she, as Edward Said suggests, 'crosses over, abandons fixed positions.'[22] She is a traveller and migrant because she conceives her life as an endless voyage, a prismatic passing through new things and being passed through by them, never reaching the promised land upon which to build a temple and never seeking to call a given part of the world her home. Ramòn Soto-Crespo reads the conclusion of the story as 'the narrator's acknowledging a fear of becoming possessed by her own allegory' — the decaying penis of Ovando which figures 'his dissemination of death and destruction' — and observes that her Carib voice 'finally fades — 'exhausted' — coincident with the spread of illness during conquest'. Soto-Crespo ties this mourning for the deaths produced by conquest to the death of Kincaid's brother from AIDS-related illness, thus arguing that 'the death of the subaltern connects lost memories to the silences of history.'[23] 'Ovando' stages the juxtaposition Edouard Glissant so clearly articulates when he observes that the nomadism of 'the Arawak communities who navigated from island to island in the Caribbean' is opposed to the Conquistadors' arrowlike nomadism which is 'a devastating desire for settlement'; he then incisively remarks that 'neither in arrowlike nomadism nor in circular nomadism are roots valid.'[24] Indeed, the difference between Arawak/Carib and Conquistadors does not grant errancy to the former and rootedness to the latter, as Kincaid's relentlessly resistant postmodernist deconstruction of binary oppositions pointedly brings into focus. Her voice is more than an anticolonial rejection of Ovando's invasion: it is a displacement of the reversal of the logic of colonialism through deconstruction. As Spivak observes, 'the too-easy West-and-the-rest polarizations sometimes rampant in postcolonial discourse studies' are 'too much a legitimation-by-reversal of the colonial attitude itself'[25]: 'Ovando' by no means participates in this discourse. As pointedly argued by Soto-Crespo in his analysis of the theme of mourning, rather than treating mourning 'as an investment that leads to profit' (a new self or an improved identity), Kincaid's narratives consider it 'a political strategy through which a diaspora writer makes transcultural connections.'[26] I think Kincaid compels us to revise our current theories in postcolonial terms in a radically comprehensive way, and 'Ovando' unquestionably contributes to a fruitful transformation of our culture precisely by imposing a moment of crisis and of rupture upon the narrative that has first sustained colonialism and then simply rejected it without decolonializing discourse by pointing towards the articulation of an alternative way of making sense of our complex being in the world.

Patrick McGrath underlines that the ingredients of the gothic genre are violence, death, blackness, and monstrosity and that its final point is 'an air, a tone, an atmosphere, a tendency,' because evil is not only the dream of the wicked but 'the mad dream' of all 'to be dreamt in a thousand forms.'[27] As Kathy Acker suggests in her story, 'The Beginning of the Life of Rimbaud,' it is the evil that forces us to move 'into the imaginary' where 'the infinity and clarity of desire [make] normal society's insanity disappear.'[28] The narrator in 'Ovando' moves us into the imaginary to make us clearly see what being enslaved signifies, to make us feel with the Carib woman that Ovando 'was horrible on a scale I did not even know existed before' ('O' 76), and to show us that his 'divine' ('O' 76) actions are conducible to the imaginary magic wand (his finger) tracing a line on his map: 'at that moment the world broke' ('O' 77). At that moment, the narrator's 'flat' world in which one's 'humanity' can be seen is taken over by Ovando's 'round' world; his magic words, 'My Sheer Might!' swallow up 'everything in their path' ('O' 79) and 'in that moment, I, my world, and everything in it became Ovando's thralls' ('O' 80). And this is how Ovando comes to 'live constantly in night' ('O' 82) and 'everything that could trace its lineage to me became nothing to Ovando' ('O' 83). Kincaid concludes by stating the narrator's exhaustion and consequent incapacity to judge 'so that his sins do not obsess and so possess me' ('O' 83). My reading here departs from Soto-Crespo's: in the narrator's exhaustion I see her victory rather than her submission to the death drive imposed by conquest. Unlike Devon in *My Brother*, who remains a subaltern throughout his marginalized life, the Carib woman narrator in 'Ovando', just like Kincaid herself, refuses confrontation with the colonizer on the imposed rhetorical ground but not for this reason is she left incapable of judgment and critical elaboration. Her point of view on Ovando's evil and the reduction of the colonized to nothingness is fully articulated and captured in the figuration of his self-love 'beyond measure' ('O' 82). The Carib woman's story keeps triggering Kincaid's writing and thinking precisely because her storytelling turned Ovando's deadly power into the story of his death. Just like Joan Anim-Addo, who refuses to bury Aphra Behn's Imoinda in silence,[29] Kincaid's deeper and deeper personal and historical making sense of her being in the world as a woman of Carib and African ancestry from the Caribbean breaks the silence into which colonialism has confined the subaltern to remind us that formerly enslaved Caribbean women did survive their holocaust and thus their voices must participate in the making of this history.

'On Seeing England for the First Time' (1991)[30]

The narrator of 'On Seeing England for the First Time' writes history with cutting irony and provides a powerful postcolonial commentary on the quincentennial's emphasis on Columbus's voyage of discovery. Kincaid's venture into history thus becomes rather a voyage of 'recovery.'

One Columbian phrase — quite possibly second only in importance to the Admiral's celebrated claim that the world is round — is a figuration of the 'otro mundo' as a nipple on the swelling breast of the world.[31] The recovery of this image has become the focus of feminist socio-cultural readings of the Columbian texts of discovery. Among these is Margarita Zamora's insightful 'Abreast of Columbus: Gender and Discovery,' which provides the Columbian grounding, as it were, for my own reading of Kincaid's story.[32]

Zamora observes that in Columbian writing, the dichotomy Spaniard-Indian is ideologized in terms of the dualist opposition feminine-masculine and is articulated through the rhetorical feminization of the term *Indian* that is contrasted to the masculine term Spaniard. In the process, the sign *Indies* is subjected to two seemingly contradictory operations: one of denigration and one of idealization. It is in this way that Columbus's dialectics inscribes 'the other world' as feminine within Western culture. Thus, 'the other world' becomes assimilated, annihilated by a discourse incapable of letting difference be, and powerful enough to obliterate the autonomy of otherness. Columbian texts of discovery interpret, rather than describe, difference. They co-opt the new cultures into a political economy which defines otherness in terms of an identity related to sameness. Hence, everything gets reduced to the dichotomy of masculine and feminine, in which the latter is granted only an exchange value. Zamora's analysis demonstrates that such discourse inscribes 'the other world' as feminine within a patriarchal culture which equates femininity to exploitability. In other words, the essay successfully shows how exploitation is determined and justified by a gendered epistemological politics.

Kincaid's texts provide a devastating subversion of Columbian hermeneutics not simply by reversing Columbus's gender-specific view, and not even by opposing the voice of the colonies to that of the empire. The previous discussion has already underlined how her voice is unquestionably anti-colonial and anti-patriarchal, but more precisely and incisively, I contend, hers is a voice that corrodes Columbian discourse because it situates her anti-colonial and anti-patriarchal stance within a radical critique of the binary logocentrism that also constitutes the grounding of the concept *gender*. She expresses the voice of the decolonialized subject who is journeying back and forth between empires and colonies of the past and the present, always refusing to adopt the language of either the vanquished or the victors and yet never pretending to be both, and thereby dissolving their difference. Her repetitive logic spins a thread that adds and modifies, but never rules out its previous positions; it demonstrates the political vitality of a feminist thought whose power is pathos, and which consists of knowing — as Rosi Braidotti claims we should — that all knowledge rests on affective and corporeal, which is to say libidinal ground.[33] Kincaid's critique of that social thought which is dependent upon the dichotomy empire or colonies, and upon the opposition centre or periphery, is counterpointed by her relentless rejection of the dualistic vision that derives from accepting *gender* as a hermeneutical concept.

Columbus's voyages were of discovery (from the Latin *discooperire*) in that he took off the veil, the mask, of something not known before, something which never belonged to him and which he must strip off in order to grasp and comprehend. His voyages were of possession — the rape of America[34] — also because his rhetoric adapted the new reality to his pre-existing ideas and words. Kincaid's voyages, in contradiction, are of recovery (from the Latin *recuperare*) in that she gains back something she previously had — her right to be a non-identity, a prismatic subjectivity. Hers are voyages of cross-cultural encounters, for example, of Lucy's. As such they do not require a discourse of inscription, as suggested by Trinh Minh-ha,[35] but are grounded instead on the endless process of re-naming the world in order to un-name it.

Literally and figuratively, Kincaid's voyages are voyages of recovery: her heroines go from the colonies to the centres of the empire — New York and London — in order to 're-depart' — as Trinh Min-Ha would put it — from the colonies after having recovered the colonial view, in a continuous process. Trinh's definition helps us to understand the significance of Kincaid's voyages: 'Re-departure: the pain and frustration of having to live a difference that has no name and too many names already.' Kincaid's naming is always a process of simultaneously re-naming and un-naming; her identity, effaced for so long in order to survive, must today be named first, must declare, as Trinh says, 'solidarity among the hyphenated people of the Diaspora.' By this she means that identity can dare say its plurality, that identity can be redefined as 'the necessity of re-naming so as to un-name.'[36]

Kincaid's commitment to infinite progress — where 'infinite' undermines linearity and rationality — and her spatial-emotional movement between advancement and regression make the name of Lucy Josephine Potter different from, and not other than the name Christopher

Columbus. Such distinction is the fundamental mark of a discourse that refuses to articulate the other side of the same coin. In fact, the Admiral thought it was pre-ordained that he should be the carrier of Christ (Christoferens); moreover, in Spanish he was Colòn, the populator, while the name Columbus recalled the Holy Spirit. Thus, by virtue of his name, his quest became the product of a celestially-revealed certainty that he was the designated instrument of a providential design to locate the Earthly Paradise. In addition, his act of naming the new discoveries was always performed as a baptismal or conversionary rite underlining the redemptive purpose of his enterprise.[37] But it was proper of Christian eschatology, as Greenblatt points out, to assume a linear destiny in which the whole world would be consumed by fire and sword before a celestial age would dawn.[38]

Kincaid, on the contrary, is fully conscious of the devastating consequences of this attitude, and she makes this clear in 'On Seeing England for the First Time' when she declares with lapidary concision: 'the idea Christopher Columbus had was more powerful than the reality he met so the reality he met died' ('SE' 37). This sentence casts light on her incredible capacity to view Columbian naming ironically in *Lucy*. With loud laughter, she shows that the colonized woman does not speak so as to respond to a figuration of the world that has oppressed and excluded her; rather, she speaks to do away with that episteme and start re/un-thinking the world anew. Lucy puts it precisely in terms of intellectual skills, when she observes that Columbus's task of naming 'would have killed a thoughtful person, but he went on to live a very long life' (*L* 135). The difference between the patriarchal and the feminist position vis-à-vis language, and hence reality, is not a switch in point of view, nor a shift from centre to margin. The process of de-westernization that the contemporary episteme is undergoing is actually another Copernican revolution presenting us with a vastly altered world. The un-telling of the stories of marginality recovers marginality as a condition of the centre, as a displacement involving the invention of new forms of subjectivities and implying the continuous renewal of critical work.

I suggest that displacing as a living in-between, as a way of surviving, is creatively expressed in Kincaid's works by the act of writing 'sentences.' A sentence (from the Latin *sentire*) is a feeling: it is an encounter, a passion, an identity which exists for a moment and then becomes, like Lucy, 'a great big blur' — a sentence is Lucy, a corporeal intelligence, a 'body that matters', to paraphrase Judith Butler.[39] A sentence is also that which Annie John writes under the picture of a chained Columbus in her textbook: 'So the Great Man Can No Longer Just Get Up and Go' (*AJ* 78). She thus captures in one gesture the relationship between patriarchy and colonialism: she attacks the explorer with the very same words that her mother used to criticize her own father, that is, with the words of women's resistance against patriarchy.

But it is probably 'On Seeing England for the First Time' which best enhances the complex significance of Kincaid's focus on 'sentences' in her writings. Like Lucy, the speaking-I of this essay discusses 'the space between the idea of something and its reality'; she observes that it is 'always wide and deep and dark' and that, although initially empty, it gets 'filled up with obsession or desire or hatred or love' ('SE' 37). Kincaid's subaltern subjects inhabit this in-between Foucauldian space and speak the feelings that fill it. In this piece, the first England 'seen' is 'an idea'- pure language, a map on which the country looks like 'a leg of mutton'; the words 'Made in England' printed on almost everything; phrases such as 'having troubling thoughts at twilight' ('SE' 34), which are baffling and preposterous in a tropical country where day and night alternate abruptly, just as incongruous as her father's felt hat or a big British breakfast in a hot climate. By the time the England 'seen' has finally become a reality, the in-between space has become so filled with hatred that Kincaid writes: 'I wished every sentence, everything I knew, that began with England, would end with 'and then it all died; we don't know how, it just all died'' ('SE' 40).

The quotation foregrounds the complex character of Kincaid's interpretation of the world, a complexity which allows no simple reversal of imperialistic, racist and sexist rhetoric. It is the prismatic validity of the word *sentence* together with its facticity that enhances the significance of Kincaid's un-writing. A 'sentence' is 'everything' she knows of England, an overwhelming 'idea' that is nevertheless the reality in Antigua, a country reduced to 'conquests, subjugation, humiliation, enforced amnesia' ('SE' 36). Yet, all she juxtaposes it with is another sentence: her wish 'that it all died.' The comparison shows the abyss existing not so much between word and world — since human beings can only inhabit the space between language and reality — but rather the abyss between a sentence that has a force behind it and one that is powerless. This fundamental difference is best illustrated by the observation that:

I may be capable of prejudice, but my prejudices have no weight to them, my prejudices have no force behind them, my prejudices remain opinions, my prejudices remain my personal opinions. . . . The people I come from are powerless to do evil on grand scale. ('SE' 40)

In addition, there is also the 'reality' of England after her voyage, which is described as 'a jail sentence' ('SE' 40).

Significantly, it is at the moment when she sees the cliffs of Dover that she realizes the need to rid herself of all these sentences and recover the strength for a re-departure:

The white cliffs of Dover, when finally I saw them, were cliffs, but they were not white; you would only call them that if the word 'white' meant something special to you; they were dirty and they were steep, the correct height from which all my views of England, starting with the map before me in my classroom and ending with the trip I had just taken, should jump and die and disappear forever. ('SE' 40)

Thus in a very short piece of storytelling Kincaid powerfully exemplifies the need for a postcolonial rewriting of history and redefinition of subjectivity.

My Garden (Book): (1999)

My Garden (Book): seems to stand apart from Kincaid's other writings. As soon as the book is lifted from the shelves reserved for manuals of gardening, however, it appears evident that its pages offer a further articulation of her most profoundly existential and political concerns. My claim is that this is indeed Kincaid's book — the book that gives body and memory to her autobiographical voice located in the present context and that conjugates personal identity with collective needs.[40] And precisely because this book is indeed *also* a practical manual for gardeners, it powerfully argues for a materialist, pragmatic philosophical articulation of cognitive, embodied subjectivity and social policy. I consider My Garden (Book): as Kincaid's most thorough articulation to date of what Gayatri Spivak has termed 'transnational literacy.'[41] In its pages, Kincaid offers a redefinition of the concept garden which displays the thoughts of a subject resisting the demand to be either native informant or hybrid globalist; instead, this redefinition engages the 'cultivation of contradictory, indeed aporetic, practical acknowledgement' on which 'a basis of a decolonization of the mind' is founded.[42] Thus she provides a redefinition of the garden framed in a postcolonial voice that is critical of postcolonial reason, and I find that her definition of gardening stands as an exemplary sense-making of the globalized contemporary world: her voice inhabits the aporia between the memory of an identity which has been subjected to historical discrimination and the impossible but necessary dream of a future undivided humanity. In addition, it expresses a strong resistance to the neo-imperialist representation of globalization as a New World Order in which the agency of capitalism determines an international division of labour replicating without a difference the colonial binary, First versus Third World. On the contrary, Kincaid's voice forcefully demonstrates that '[t]he migrant is First World space' and articulates the contemporary without erasing this complexity.[43] As she puts it: 'I was of the conquered class' (*MG* 120) and 'I have joined the conquesting class: who else could afford this garden — a garden in which I grow things that it would be much cheaper to buy at the store? My feet are (so to speak) in two worlds' (*MG* 123).

The title *My Garden (Book):* is framed as a dictionary entry, where the subsumption of garden to book underlines the impossibility of separating nature from culture, and the text that follows the colon satisfies our expectations for a definition of, **Species**: *garden* (**Genus**: *book*). Unsurprisingly, this is given an extremely complex description which inhabits a discourse interconnecting the botanical, the philosophical, and the political. It makes it crystal clear that a metaphor is a cognitive and not a linguistic entity,[44] thus giving force to Kincaid's careful attention to the relation between language and understanding in her whole work. The chapter titles point in this complex direction: for example, we move from 'Wisteria' and 'The Garden in Winter' in the first Part, through 'The Old Suitcase' indicating England and 'To Name is to Possess' in the second Part, to 'Where to Begin' and 'The Garden in Eden' in the third Part. However, this movement should not suggest that the story progresses from botany, through colonial history, to postcolonial subjectivity; these issues are so intricately joined that chapters do not provide any ordered partition. The definition of the garden/book, consequently, takes us beyond scientific taxonomical classifications, historical analysis, and epistemological inquiry to explore the political implications of the mutual interactions among these.

As a gardening manual, *My Garden (Book):* shows Jamaica Kincaid the gardener offering practical suggestions and useful information for growing plants and flowers, such as where to buy the best seeds and bushes. An entire chapter consists of a letter to a nursery in California in which the phrase 'desirer of flora in action' (*MG* 170), referring to an appreciated nurseryowner, is coined. There are tips on how to kill bugs and slugs, and stories about foxes and rabbits disturbing her garden in which flower beds resemble 'a map of the Caribbean' (*MG* 8). There is also the admission, no doubt unusual for a gardener, that what draws her to grow plants that 'transcend the ordinary ... have a different colour from the usual ... a different shape ... come from far away' (*MG* 56) is a 'perversity' (*MG* 57). And there is even the evaluation of a number of catalogues with the observation that 'the best catalogues of any kind ... will not have any pictures' but rather 'will be full of anecdotes' (*MG* 62). This statement emphasizes Kincaid's poetics, wholly articulated in *The Autobiography of My Mother*, according to which a narrative which inhabits the border between the real and the fictional is closer to the truth than photographic representations of the world.

As a historical study on the significance of gardening, *My Garden (Book):* reveals Kincaid the writer exploring the implications of the garden as appropriation and colonization of the wild world: for instance, she entertains the question of 'the relationship between gardening and conquest' (*MG*116) and wonders when exactly the Mexican cocoxochtil went to Europe to be hybridized and renamed dahlia after a Swedish botanist (see *MG* 118). Then, in the chapter entitled 'The Glasshouse,' she defines 'unusual' the idea of this enclosure, as unusual as 'leaving your own native (European) climate and living in places native to other people whom you cannot stand' and associates such ideas with 'dominators, the English people, their love, their need to isolate, name, objectify, possess various parts, people, and things in the world' (*MG* 143). In this context, thus, the information that on the author's night table sits 'a large stack of books and all of them concern the Atlantic slave trade and how the world in which I live sprang from it' (*MG* 64), does not strike the readers as unusual. The overpowering legacy of colonial history is not only pertinent; it also produces a cutting definition of the topic of the book: 'a garden is the most useless of creations' (*MG* 111), followed by the observation that botany 'cannot be eaten' nor 'taken to the market' (*MG* 139). Gardening is associated with 'prosperity' but, unlike a 'painting or a piece of sculpture,' it does not challenge the temporality of being; on the contrary, 'time is its enemy' (*MG* 111). These observations are more effective because they are framed within a discourse which does not aim at separating nature from culture, and Third from First World according to an oppositional moralizing logic; thus, gardening is juxtaposed to agriculture, which can certainly be eaten and taken to the market, but the latter is not for this reason more pleasing to the people in Antigua who, precisely because of agricultural interests, were deported from Africa and enslaved in the Americas (*MG* 139). Similarly, Kincaid contrasts Tsitsi Dangarembga with Henry James in a sharp comparative reading of their descriptions of gardens (see *MG* 114-117), where the Zimbabwean writer explains how the idea of 'planting for joy ... for merrier reasons than the chore of keeping breath in the body' was initially 'strange' to her and how it became then a 'liberation' (*MG* 115). Thus James's 'rich, rich, rich' description, which 'could have been written only by a person who comes from a place where the wealth of the world is like a skin' (*MG* 116), is redefined, decolonialized — appropriated for 'liberation' — rather than simply rejected. By placing herself in this text not only as the writer but also as a reader of other texts, Kincaid explicitates the act of reading as an allegory for unverifiable truth which only a negotiation between the reader and writer can temporarily and relatively approach.[45] Likewise, scientific taxonomical classifications which are so appealing to botanists in the First World always 'longing' for unusual, exotic 'blooms' (*MG* 201) are juxtaposed to names given to plants for their use by people in the Third World where, she claims, plants 'would fall into the category Household Management' (*MG* 119). In fact, cocoxochtil means water pipes, because Mexicans used to cure urinary tract infections with dahlias (see MG 118), and in Antigua the plants used to make tea for inducing abortion is known as abortion bush (see *MG* 119). Nevertheless, and despite being associated with colonial conquest, the botanists' incurable 'longing' for new species is also passionately shared by Kincaid. Not only does she take a 'plant hunting' journey to China with a group of 'real botanists ... in the grip of their passion' (*MG* 193), but she also participates in their excitement over collecting exotic seeds, i.e., for colonizing through 'naming of things which is so crucial to possession — a spiritual padlock with the key thrown irretrievably away-that it is a murder' (*MG* 122). However, one fundamental difference in her passion for gardening marks a postcolonial shift of the episteme: if in the early pages she defines gardening as an attraction for things 'to come' (*MG* 85), by the end of the book the projection towards the future is rendered more complex by the declaration that 'memory is a gardener's real palette; memory as it summons up the past, memory as it shapes the present, memory as it dictates the future' (*MG* 218-9). Kincaid's garden is thus redefined as the place of Morrisonian re-memorying and this should not surprise us after the gardener's unconditional declaration of love for 'all places of transition' (*MG* 202) and after the description of her arrangement of flower beds as a map of the Caribbean, with Hispaniola cited as exemplary of a 'misunderstanding'. In the middle of this bed, a plant of *Carpinus betulus* 'Pendula' looked 'as if it had found itself *orphaned* and in care of people who could not love it in the way it had thought appropriate in which to be loved' (*MG* 27). This shift in the significance attributed to the garden is best exemplified by Kincaid's journey to China, whose importance in the economy of the book is much greater with regards to returning home to her own garden than to collecting trophies from the plant-hunting expedition to this Other World. Incidentally, this part of the story exemplifies the political strength of this book also through the deceptively naïve remark, 'we were having delicious dinner of Chinese food (though in China it is not Chinese food, it is only food' (*MG* 192), which dismisses without appeal the habit to other difference in the globalized, multicultural village.

Finally, as epistemic meditation, *My Garden (Book):* displays Kincaid the artist intent on transforming the metaphysical image of the Garden of Eden into a flowing materialistic figuration of gardening: God freezing life into immortality in Eden and the related idea of the garden as a triumphantly ordered domestication of nature are both being metamorphosed into an ongoing activity aimed at making sense of things transient and unpredictable. The transformation affects not only the Garden of Eden, but England, the Fatherland as Eden, and the British Colony as the extension of its garden; and also the garden as botanical garden and a history of naming/possessing/domesticating large parts of the world; and finally the garden as the image of a feminine confinement into the domestic sphere, the Victorian lady in the garden. Apropos, Kincaid adamantly expresses her 'antipathy to Vita Sackville West and her garden' originated by 'the way she manages to be oblivious to the world' and accentuates that on the contrary 'the world cannot be left out of the garden' (*MG* 82). By dismantling this entire set of associations, Kincaid herself becomes the gardener in a space that resembles what Alice Walker has termed the 'mothers' gardens,' a cultural space that privileges memory over development.[46] In the chapter 'The Garden in Eden' she tells how the ideal eventually 'turned out into the world as I have come to know it' (*MG* 221): Eden 'turned wrong,' because

> the owner grew tired of the rigid upkeep of His creation (and I say His on purpose), of the rules that could guarantee its continued perfect existence, and most definitely tired of that design of the particular specimen (Tree of Life, Tree of Knowledge) as the focal point in the center ... and the occupants (Adam and then Eve), too, seemed to have grown tired of the demands of the Gardener and most certainly of His ideas of what the garden ought to be ... this layout became boring to them after a while, this layout ... had all the sadness that comes with satisfaction. (*MG* 223-4)

This new garden evolved from Eden is not a mausoleum; as Adrienne Rich reminds us, the migrant woman representing poetry never rests on the known, never builds a temple, nor settles in the newly-found promised land.[47] In this book, Kincaid expresses prismatic subjectivity poetically as a gardener, 'not a stable being ... not a model of consistency' (*MG* 224), who is at home in a place that 'repeats itself all the time and will advance only so long as human history and all that it entails moves along also' (*MG* 61). Within the flux of such moving along, the question 'What to do?' is always kept alive; it holds together the narrative by a subject who joins knowledge and experience and who reiterates her declaration of love for 'the rush of things' (*MG* 24), for the messiness of living, in which the moment of perfection is not isolated from what comes after and before it. What is being emphasized is the temporality of being, which is forcefully described as the capability of making 'the rational way imbued with awe' (*MG* 16). Such being can feel joy for the process, not the completion of living, and is thus at home in the activity of gardening, the space inhabited by continuous striving rather than final accomplishment. The garden thus re-defined rather than figuring the mastering of nature by human culture is the proper ecological habitat of the prismatic subject, satisfied with what 'must never completely satisfy' (*MG* 220), with 'an arrangement of things carefully attended to, so that it ... looks neglected, abandoned' (*MG* 227). Therefore, as a conclusion to her exploration of this complex epistemic space, the prismatic voice can articulate her utopic social vision and triumphantly declare her love for living in a shared state of becoming and limited comprehension. Her dream is to accept 'that there are some things we cannot take because we just don't understand them' and to collectively enjoy the unpredictability of being in the world: 'I am in a state of constant discomfort and I like this state so much I would like to share it' (*MG* 227).

Her being at home in this fractal dimension implies a definition of home; the chapter entitled 'The House' devotes considerable space to this definition and should be seriously regarded. In the first chapters introducing her garden, after pointing out that she 'can easily describe' her house but not her home (*MG* 28), Kincaid proceeds to wonder whether her present house with a garden has indeed been made into a home (*MG* 46). We understand that it has, because this large house in Vermont — as she points out, 'Americans take up at least twenty times as much of everything as they need' (*MG* 37) — 'looks quite like the outside in which I grew up. The outside in which I grew up had an order to it, but this order had to be restored at the beginning of each day' (*MG* 43). She wishes that someone had given her and her family 'a recipe for how to make a house a home,' for which she provides the following ground-breaking definition:

> a home being a place in which the mystical way of maneuvering through the world in an ethical way, a way universally understood to be honorable and universally understood to be static and universally understood to be the way we would all want it to be, carefully balanced between our needs and the needs of other people. (*MG* 48)

In the same chapter, the question 'Is this a home?' (*MG* 46) referring to her house is effectively and equally originally answered by telling an anecdote which is exemplary of the definition provided in the above quotation. This is about the time her four-year-old daughter Annie interrupted the conversations of her parents asking them to explain what 'a homophobe' was (*MG* 47). The straightforward, clear explanation offered by her father provides a superb example of how space — either the domestic space within one's house or the social space constituting one's nation, 'home' meaning both — can be 'carefully balanced between our needs and the needs of other people.' Home, for Kincaid, is neither a shelter from the outside world nor a space shared by people who unquestionably agree with one another; rather, it designates a space which is shareable because it is where negotiations among individuals continuously occur. To me, this is one of the numerous remarks that illustrate how this book translates epistemological inquiry into political thinking, and identity politics into a politics of the collectivity. Defining home as the place where 'others' are accepted without being othered and where difference is explained without being moralistically ranked is a political statement of poignant significance for the present postcolonial globalized world, in which 'the others' are increasingly being encountered 'at home' in the global village. Kincaid's prismatic voice is always situated within the power networks of contemporary society and always attempting to influence them. Since sexuality is homophobically regulated by such forces, the plain acceptance by Kincaid's nuclear heterosexual family of homosexuality as a perfectly normal life-style is significant, especially because this acceptance does not bear any mark of linguistic difference. Even more clearly unmarked is the reiteration of the equal social and rhetorical treatment reserved to hetero- and homosexual marriages, as described in the following episode about her journey to China:

> Dan (that is, Daniel Hinkley) and I were rooming together; I had requested it because he is my friend, the only person I knew on this expedition, and I felt very safe (he would like me no matter what) with him. This arrangement, of Dan and me, a man and a woman who were not married to each other, caused a small wave of disapproval; but Dan and I are both married — to other people, he to someone named Robert and I to someone named Allen, and we both had in common that we think of our marriages like breathing: ultimately fragile, so nothing must be done to compromise it. (MG 192)

And even this militant support of her marriage is not founded on an a-critical view of the institution of the family, as the following cutting declaration sharply underlines in conclusion to the chapter 'Spring':

> Families are a malevolent lot, no matter the permutations they make no matter the shape they take, no matter how beautiful they look, no matter the nice things they say. (MG 178)

A devastating declaration indeed, were it not placed as it is within a narration which succeeds in exposing the complexity of relations both within and outside traditional social institutions, rather than simply dismissing certain relations in favour of alternative ones. *My Garden (Book):* is dedicated to Kincaid's children 'with blind, instinctive, and confused love' and expresses her love for her husband Allen, her admiration for him as a father and her longing for him as a partner while she is in China. It never indulges in drawing a romantic picture of the happy family; love even within this heavily predetermined institution is rather critically articulated as the continuous expression of political negotiations. What stands between Kincaid's 'blind, instinctive, and confused love' for her children and a marriage that is like 'breathing' on the one hand and the thoughtless, Tupperware-sealed, 'perfect union' promoted by Hollywood narratives on the other is gardening, which 'has no serious intention ... only series of doubts upon series of doubts' (*MG* 15) and a passionate love for

> the rush of things, the thickness of things, everything condensed as it is happening, long after it has happened so that any attempt to understand it will become like an unravelling of a large piece of cloth that had been laid flat and framed and placed as a hanging on a wall and, even then, expected to stand for something. (*MG* 24)

Thus, politically, Kincaid's garden/book expresses the incompleteness, undecidability and complexity of everyday life as well as the need for things 'expected to stand for something'; the prism in these pages is immersed into the present context and Kincaid's actual location as a successful writer living in the US. Her 'feet are (so to speak) in two worlds' (*MG* 123), a privileged condition, not at all assimilable to that of the migrant worker whose feet are required (so to speak) to choose between two worlds. By acknowledging her class-related privilege, Kincaid addresses how complex issues of citizenship are in a globalized context.[48] Clearly, by virtue of her present social and intellectual status, although an 'alien' in the US and although black in a racist culture, Kincaid enjoys full transnational citizenship, including the right to 'other' those who have othered her. She explains this clearly in the following statement: 'I am living comfortably in a place that I am not from, enjoying my position of visitor, enjoying my position of not-the-native, enjoying especially

the privilege of being able to make sound judgements about the Other'
(*MG* 67). Both synchronically and diachronically — gardening and self-
positioning in relation to the geopolitics of a globalized economy and to
the legacy of colonial history — her privileged prism reflects an intricate
network of forces. As a result, the description of **Species:** *garden* (**Genus**:
book) carries deep ethical implications, related to the prism's social agency
in and to its cultural understanding of contemporary global hegemony
as well as to its own local historical victimization. In her 'Preface' to *A
Critique of Postcolonial Reason*, Spivak argues that 'the ethics of alterity' is
not 'a politics of identity' and suggests that, in retrospect, she would like
to add Kincaid's *Lucy* to her analysis. In my next chapter, I concentrate
my reading of *Lucy* precisely on the blurring of the protagonist's name at
the end, which Spivak sharply points out is a claiming of the 'right/
responsibility of loving, denied to the subject that wishes to choose agency
from victimage.'[49] *My Garden (Book):* elaborates this position in the form
of the philosophical essay rather than the fictional story by situating the
prismatic, blurred identity, of her younger years into the present,
demanding from her responsibility, answerability, and accountability, and
thus widening the scope of her original critique of mere identity politics
into the elaboration of a politics of the collectivity and of solidarity. Her
poetics open more and more explicitly to a discourse of love, allowing
her prism to inhabit embodied desire and to accept alterity, because she
has fully accepted herself. Her extended discussion of her own bitchiness
amusingly indicates this: she refers to her 'monumentally rude and
insulting behaviour' (*MG* 200) and, in response to one of her fellow
travellers' complaint that she was always bitching, she underlines that
'bitchin' can't be done by someone who isn't a bitch' (*MG* 189).

    That loving thus relationally conceived is an act of extreme political
impact is made clear once again by Spivak in an unusually — but perhaps
necessarily — lyrical, deeply passionate passage:

> Indeed, it is my conviction that the internationality of ecological justice
> in the impossible, undivided world of which one must dream, in view
> of the impossibility of which one must work, obsessively, cannot be
> reached by invoking any of the so-called religions of the world because
> the history of their greatness is too deeply imbricated in the narrative
> of the ebb and flow of power .... I have no doubt that we must learn to
> learn from the original practical ecological philosophies of the world.

Again, I am not romanticizing, liberation theology does not romanticize every Christian. We are talking about using the strongest mobilizing discourse in the world in a certain way, for the globe, not merely for the Fourth World uplift. .... This learning can only be attempted through the supplementation of collective effort by love. What deserves the name of love is an effort — over which one has no control yet at which one must not strain — which is slow, attentive on both sides — how does one win the attention of the subaltern without coercion or crisis? — mindchanging on both sides, at the possibility of an unascertainable ethical singularity that is not ever a sustainable condition. The necessary collective efforts are to change laws, relations of production, systems of education, and health care. But without the mind-changing one-on-one responsible contact, nothing will stick.[50]

Supplementing 'collective effort by love' is thus the recipe for uprooting the episteme which imposes a choice between dominant and subaltern, native informant and mimic voice. In a space opened up by the interplay of lyric and narrative, the possibility of making sense of a prismatic being in the contemporary, globalized world is figured in positive terms. Without resorting to the assumption of cultural identity for justifying the existence of collectivity, the prism relates to difference without othering it, victimizing it or being victimized by it. As I suggest in my third chapter, this act of solidarity and expression of mature independence of the prismatic self is fully articulated in *The Autobiography of My Mother*, *My Brother*, and *Mr. Potter*. In her chapter 'The Garden I Have in Mind,' Kincaid's description of her political project, of what Spivak calls 'the undivided world of which one must dream' is most incisive. More so, with the ending of the book in mind, where she declares that she likes 'so much' this 'state of constant discomfort' that she 'would like to share it' (*MG* 229):

But we who covet our neighbor's garden must finally return to our own, with all its ups and downs, its disappointments, its rewards. We come to it with a blindness, plus a jumble of feelings that mere language (as far as I can see) seems inadequate to express ...

I shall never have the garden I have in mind, but that for me is the joy of it; certain things can never be realized and so all the more reason to attempt them. A garden, no matter how good it is, must never completely satisfy. The world as we know it, after all, began in a very good garden, a completely satisfying garden — Paradise — but after a while the owner and the occupants wanted more. (*MG* 220)

Notes

1   For example, Audre Lorde, 'Poetry is Not a Luxury' in *Sister Outsider*, Trumansburgh, NY: Crossing Press, 1984, and Adrienne Rich, 'Tourism and Promised Lands' in *What is Found There*, New York: Norton, 1993, provide examples of lyrical political philosophy which are as powerful as Jamaica Kincaid's *A Small Place*.

2   For a clear presentation in feminist terms of the fractal as an effective figuration of contemporary complexity and subjectivity, I refer to Elena Bougleux's paper given at the seminar *Raccontar(si) III*, Prato, 2003 (proceedings forthcoming).

3   See Caren Kaplan, *Questions of Travel*, Durham: Duke University Press, 1996.

4   Gayatri C. Spivak, 'The Politics of Translation' in Michèle Barrett and Anne Phillips, eds. *Destabilizing Theory: Contemporary Feminist Debates*, Palo Alto, CA: Stanford University Press, 1992: 177-200, p. 192.

5   Gayatri C. Spivak, *Outside in the Teaching Machine*, New York: Routledge, 1993, p. 15.

6   This is a revised version of my review essay 'Jamaica Kincaid's Political Place,' originally published in *Caribana* 1/1990: 93-103 and of my article 'Jamaica Kincaid and the Resistance to Canons,' in Carole Boyce Davies and Elaine Savory Fido, eds., *Out of the Kumbla: Caribbean Women and Literature*, Trenton: Africa World Press, 1990: 345-354.

7   Jack Forbes, *Africans and Native Americans*, Urbana: University of Illinois Press, 1993. By 'true American' Forbes intends the people of mixed blood who have repopulated the Americas in post-colonial times. Forbes's important research on race corrects the assumption that in the Caribbean region, the southern US and the coastal mainland of South America, Native Americans were replaced by Africans and Europeans in the course of colonial history. 'What has in fact happened,' he pointedly demonstrates, 'is that American survivors and African survivors (because huge numbers of Africans also died in the process) have merged together to create the basic modern populations of much of the Greater Caribbean and adjacent mainland regions' (p. 270). His study underlines the extent to which racism has forced a complex ethnic heritage into arbitrarily simplistic categories. Forbes's taxonomical research is well tuned with Jamaica Kincaid's critical definition of race throughout her works.

8   Moira Ferguson, *Jamaica Kincaid: Where the Land Meets the Body*, University of Virginia Press, 1994, p. 80.

9   Laura Niesen de Abruna, 'Family Connections: Mother and Mother Country in the Fiction of Jean Rhys and Jamaica Kincaid' in Susheila Nasta, ed., *Motherlands: Black Women's Writing from Africa, the Caribbean and South Asia*, London: The Women's Press, 1991: 257-289, defines *A Small Place* as a series of 'anti-colonialist essays' (p. 277). Diane Simmons, *Jamaica Kincaid*, New York: Twayne, 1994, defines *A Small Place* as an 'essay' which marks a 'most profound shift' (p. 135) in Kincaid's work. Moira Ferguson's *Jamaica Kincaid: Where the Land Meets the Body* (1994)

insightfully defines this 'text' as 'counterknowledge' (p. 100) and appreciates it as 'a weapon for social change that privileges black women as agents of change and loci of contradiction' (p. 94), capable of 'challeng[ing] hypocrisy' and dispers[ing] the pernicious postcolonial gaze' with its 'confrontational style'; most importantly and in perfect tune with my own reading, she also finds the 'text' capable of 'pry[ing] open creative possibilities for a new syncretic order, a new epistemological reading of a critical historical era, usually coded as the transition form British colonialism to national independence' (p. 101); finally, she defines as 'deftly fashioned yet deceptively simple' the technical strategies which 'enhance this complicated matrix of meaning' (p. 102). Susan Sniader Lanser's forceful statement for a global feminist comparativist critical approach, 'Compared to What? Global Feminism, Comparatism, and the Master's Tools' in Margaret Higonnet, ed., *Borderwork: Feminist Engagements with Comparative Literature*, Ithaca: Cornell UP, 1994: 280-300, significantly identifies *A Small Place* as the exemplary 'brilliantly disturbing book' (p. 280) capable of unsettling "influence' studies in comparative literature' (p. 285) and imposing instead a confrontation with new definitions of theories and texts, language and culture, nation and subjectivity. Lizabeth Paravisini-Gebert, *Jamaica Kincaid: A Critical Companion*, Westport, CT: Greenwood Press, 1999, considers it as a departure from Kincaid's previous fiction 'in tone and approach' (p. 31) and defines it as a 'thematic breakthrough' (p. 118) which relies on a 'mature voice of denunciation' (p. 31), and observes that without 'the fictional façade as mediating space' the themes which are otherwise shared, are here 'distilled through anger and presented more forthrightly' (p. 32). Isabel Hoving, *In Praise of New Travelers: Reading Caribbean Migrant Women's Writing*, Stanford: Stanford UP, 2001, also focuses on Kincaid's anger and describes *A Small Place* as 'shaped as a long essay' (p. 187). Suzanne Gauch, 'A *Small Place*: Some Perspectives on the Ordinary' in *Callaloo*, 25:3 (Summer 2002): 910-19, defines it as an 'essay' which is 'neither quite travel narrative nor theory' and which 'addresses otherness by rejecting it in favor of ordinariness' (p. 910), which in turn is defined in terms similar to Bhabha's concept of the liminal and Spivak's suggestion to speak *to* rather than *for* another in order to negotiate a possible representation of the subaltern (p. 918). From a different disciplinary perspective, Nadine Dolby, 'A *Small Place*: Jamaica Kincaid and a Methodology of Connection' in *Qualitative Inquiry*, 9:1 (2003): 57-73, emphasizes Kincaid's epistemological break by arguing that the essay places at the centre of its analysis global connections thus forcing upon us a shifted perspective in ethnographic inquiry.

10   Early reviewers underline the rage which characterizes *A Small Place* but mostly focus on the first part of the book. Diane Simmons, *Jamaica Kincaid*, New York: Twayne, 1994, has rightly criticized this colour-blind reading (see pp.135-42); more recently, Isabel Hoving, *In Praise of New Travelers*, has further analyzed anger in Kincaid concentrating on this book; her interpretation relies on Audre Lorde's 'The Uses of Anger: Women Responding to Racism' in *Sister Outsider*: 124-33, to show that here Kincaid 'uses the master's voice in a satanical way, disturbing it by means of the colonized's speech' and resulting in 'the decolonization of discourse' (p. 202).

11   Moira Ferguson, *Where the Land Meets the Body*, pp. 84 and 83.

12   Moira Ferguson, *Where the Land Meets the Body*, p. 98.

13   Suzanne Gauch, '*A Small Place*: Some Perspectives on the Ordinary,' argues that equating racism with impoliteness 'personalizes the crime rather than ignoring it' (p. 914); by treating colonialism as a discourse on manners, Kincaid not only humanizes the English but also grants Antiguans the agency to resist the discourse of race (see p. 915).

14   Epifanio San Juan, *Racial Formations/Critical Transformations: Articulations of Power in Ethnic and Racial Studies in the United States*, New Jersey, 1992, p.96

15   Moira Ferguson, *Where the Land Meets the Body*, p. 100.

16   Thomas Pynchon, *Gravity's Rainbow*, New York: Viking, 1973.

17   Moira Ferguson, *Where the Land Meets the Body*, pp. 103, 104.

18   According to Moira Ferguson, *Where the Land Meets the Body*, 'Ovando' extends *A Small Place* by giving us 'a myth of origin' (p. 132) for colonialism, showing us the ancestors of contemporary tourists; 'Antiguan people in *A Small Place* are intertextualized as Ovando's political legatees' (p. 153).

19   Moira Ferguson's *Where the Land Meets the Body* provides detailed historical background for reading this story (pp. 135-60).

20   Ramòn E. Soto-Crespo, 'Death and the Diaspora Writer: Hybridity and Mourning in the Work of Jamaica Kincaid' in *Contemporary Literature* XLIII, 2 (2002): 342-376, points out how 'the historical process of naming and renaming — a process central to techniques of imperial domination and control — created a map of the Caribbean that was so confusing as to *confound* control' (p. 349).

21   Moira Ferguson, *Where the Land Meets the Body*, p. 144.

22   Edward Said, 'Identity, Authority and Freedom' in *Reflections on Exile*, Cambridge, MASS: Harvard University Press, 2000, p. 404.

23   Ramòn Soto-Crespo, 'Death and the Diaspora Writer', p. 362.

24   Edouard Glissant, *Poetique de la Relation*, Paris: Gallimard, 1990, p.12.

25   Gayatri C. Spivak, *A Critique of Postcolonial Reason*, Cambridge: Harvard University Press, 1999, p. 39.

26   Ramòn Soto-Crespo, 'Death and the Diaspora Writer', pp. 370-1.

27   Patrick McGrath, 'Afterword' in *Conjunctions*, 14 (1989): 239-244, p. 244.

28   Kathy Acker, 'The Beginning of the Life of Rimbaud' in *Conjunctions*, 14 (1989): 150-165, p. 151.

29   Joan Anim-Addo, *Imoinda: Or She Who Will Loose Her Name* in G. Covi, ed. *Voci femminili caraibiche e interculturalità*, Trento: Dipartimento di Scienze Filologiche e Storiche, 2003: Appendix. In this opera libretto, Joan Anim-Addo re-writes Aphra Behn's *Oroonoko* from the point of view of Imoinda.

30   An earlier version of this reading appeared in Giovanna Covi, 'Jamaica Kincaid's Voyage of Recovery: The Cliffs of Dover are Not White' in Gert Buelens and Ernst Rudin, eds., *Deferring a Dream: Literary Sub-Versions of the American Columbiad*, Boston: Birkhäuser, 1994: 76-84.

31   See Christopher Columbus, 'Account of the Third Voyage to the Indies.'

32   Margarita Zamora, 'Abreast of Columbus: Gender and Discovery' in *Cultural Critique* (Winter 1990-91): 127-149.

33   See Rosi Braidotti, *Metamorphoses: Towards a Materialist Theory of Becoming*, Cambridge, UK: Polity Press, 2002.

34   One example among many is provided by the description of Guiana written in 1596 by Sir Walter Raleigh for Elizabeth I, as quoted in Myra Jehlen, *Readings at the Edge of Literature*, Chicago: University of Chicago Press, 2002, p.201.

35   See Trinh Minh-ha, *When the Moon Waxes Red: Representation, Gender and Cultural Politics*. New York: Routledge, 1991.

36   Trinh Minh-ha *When the Moon Waxes Red*, p. 14.

37   See Simon Shama, 'Full Circle' in *Guardian Weekly* (Feb 23, 1992): 26-7.

38   Stephen Greenblatt, *Marvelous Possessions: The Wonder of the New World*, Chicago: University of Chicago Press, 1991.

39   Judith Butler, *Bodies that Matter*, London: Routledge, 1993.

40   Ramòn Soto-Crespo, in his provoking discussion of a postcolonial definition of mourning as hybridity, also underlines the political rather than psychological interest in Kincaid's consideration of the garden as imperial trope; see 'Death and the Diaspora Writer.'

41   What I have in mind as I read Kincaid is Spivak's explanation, in the chapter 'Culture' of *A Critique of Postcolonial Reason* (pp. 312-421), that such literacy is not identitarian analysis, not the effort to account for more recognizably political phenomena, and not even the embrace of global hybridity; rather, it is the expression of the responsibility, answerability and accountability that, by nourishing contradictory practices of relation, concur to decolonizing the mind.

42   Gayatri C. Spivak, *A Critique of Postcolonial Reason*, p. 399.

43   Gayatri C. Spivak, *A Critique of Postcolonial Reason*, p 382.

44   See Monika Fludernik, Donald Freeman, and Maragret Freeman, 'Metaphor and Beyond: An Introduction', *Poetics Today*, 20:3 (Fall 1999): 383-96.

45   On reading in this political sense versus reading as understanding experience, which is granted a foundational referential authority, see Gayatri C. Spivak, *Death of A Discipline*, New York: Columbia University Press, 2003, p. 76.

46   Alice Walker, *In Search of Our Mothers' Gardens*, San Diego: Harcourt, 1983.

47   Adrienne Rich, 'The Woman Immigrant' in *What is Found There, Notebooks on Poetry and Politics*, New York: Norton, 1993.

48   Saskia Sassen offered a complex definition of citizenship at the Fifth European Feminist Conference 'Gender and Power' in Lund, August 2003.

49   Gayatri C. Spivak, *A Critique of Postcolonial Reason*, p. x.

50   Gayatri C. Spivak, *A Critique of Postcolonial Reason*, p. 383.

Chapter Two

Birthing Oneself: Identity On the Run
At the Bottom of the River — Annie John — Lucy

In its commitment to the pursuit of knowledge which takes the risk of subverting the very foundation of its own thinking, Kincaid's fiction is fundamentally similar to her essays. The continuous rewriting of her own life in terms of a conflictual confrontation with her mother and country goes beyond the personal claiming of her right to independence and emancipation: her individual struggle for liberation from economic and cultural restrictions vindicates not only a history of gender discrimination, racial oppression, and colonial subjugation, but also persistently dismantles the ideological foundations that have supported the imposition of sexual, racial, and imperial hierarchies in modern times. Kincaid's personal stories contribute to the creation of a new culture which resists the former colonial as well as the present neo-imperial forms of domination, both in terms of a revision of historiography and in terms of identity politics. The autobiographical work focused on her youth can be seen as written parallel to, rather than against her mother's life;[1] in Caribbean terms, her voice is that of a woman who is becoming her own mother, in order to become herself, birth herself, re-invent herself, and celebrate the creativity and continuity of birth as the ingenious potential to re-define herself in her continuously changing being in the world.[2]

Through the eyes of first a girl and later a young woman, we are being helped to conceive feminist subjectivities that, however temporary and changeable, are fully conscious of the forces of power that threaten to reduce them to subaltern positions, precisely because they are grounded on those personal and collective facts of history which cannot and should not be erased.[3] They participate in the process of 're-memory,' which allows for former oppression to turn into knowledge and empowerment and to shape present liberation and resistance;[4] and they do so by promoting an identity which never rests on the newly-found place, never turns it into a monumental, promised land.[5] In various forms, these subjectivities promote migrant, nomadic identities that keep passing from place to place, through time and places, and are in turn passed through and interrupted by their encounters with difference so that they can strategically and mimetically pass for other identities in certain contexts.[6] As they move from Antigua to the US, they articulate a transnational identity capable of expressing the maximum respect for regional historical peculiarities and of showing an incredible capacity to change in the process — indeed, these are subjectivities in continuous metamorphosis;[7] as Jessica Hagedorn would put it, Kincaid's prismatic subject is 'definitionless, identity on the run.'[8] These earlier narrations 'on the run,' like Kincaid's later (auto)biographical novels, are set 'at home' and tell about leaving 'home' or going back to visit 'home'; in the process, they radically redefine current notions of 'home' in increasingly more complex and challenging ways. 'Home' refers to the private place of one's family and thus to one's origin, as well as to the public place of one's nation; since these early stories and through her successive writings, Kincaid has drastically subverted established definitions of both family and nation,[9] thereby articulating, rather than Antigua as the place of her 'home', the various places she has inhabited as the space that her identities 'on the run' have made their 'home.'

At the Bottom of the River (1983)[10]

A 'silent voice' fulfills the task of expressing a multiplicity of voices and shaping prismatic subjectivity in the collection of short stories At the Bottom of the River. This voice, I argue, is already capable of locating herself triumphantly outside the dichotomy victor or vanquished, because, even though she expresses the powerless point of view of a very young girl, she identifies with and confronts her mother, whose position within the patriarchal-colonial system of power is ambiguous and continuously negotiable. It is through this strategy of negotiating and double-acting that the young woman learns to develop her own subjectivity.

The opening piece 'Girl' reads like a list, pounded out by the beat of drums, which provides the only comment to the message that, in a world in which 'ends' are meant to 'meet,' girls are 'bent on becoming sluts' (BR 5). A breath-taking series of imperatives and prohibitions, culminating with the direction on 'how to make ends meet' (*BR* 5), serves as a prelude to the final condemnation of the girl as 'a slut' — not surprising in a story that is almost a chronicle of a slut foretold. The practice of making ends meet is the primary target of this ferocious critique that manages to expose the very origin of sexual role division, the rational construction of an ideology of symmetry. The sound of the drums that beat within the lines nervously imparting the orders — the two-and-a-half-page story consists of a single sentence — serves as a political commentary, as a cry of protest against the predetermined destiny of the girl under patriarchal law. Repetition here serves the same function as it does in *A Small Place*.

The law of gender hierarchy is proclaimed and imposed by the mother upon the girl, whose first encounter with normative power is represented by her mother. A few elements, clearly indicated by Lizabeth Paravisini-Gebert in her thoughtful and detailed critical companion to Jamaica Kincaid,[11] emphasize that Kincaid uses the figure of the mother as the main channel not only of patriarchal but also of colonial principles, in that the model she holds up is that of the English Lady. The girl's reaction against this type of control by the mother is implied by her only two short italicized intrusions — 'but I don't sing benna on Sundays at all and never in Sunday school' (*BR* 4) and 'but what if the baker won't let me feel the bread?' (*BR* 5) — and by the mother's last lines of her overwhelmingly long sentence switching from the imperative to the interrogative.

Of particular interest is the story 'Blackness,' in which the disruption of binary oppositions is overwhelming: everything is ambiguous, multiple, and fragmented. Blackness is the night that 'falls in silence' as well as a colour of skin (*BR* 46). But above all, it is what cannot be defined: a signifier that escapes its signified by a continuous shifting, 'for I see that I cannot see' (*BR* 46). This is identity conjugated with the annihilation of the self, a celebration of a narrative 'I,' who ends its song with the words, 'I am no longer 'I'' (*BR* 52). Indeed, this is selfhood becoming subjectivity. Just like the tourist in *A Small Place* who is 'a whole person' at the price of being 'not too well equipped to look too far inward' (*SP* 16), the narrator in 'Blackness' disrupts the concept of identity as oneness, as phallic singularity, and suggests a relational prismatic subjectivity instead. Like the ambivalence of the mother's body that is One and Other at the same time (herself and the child she bears), this 'I' can say: 'the blackness cannot be separated from me but often I can stand outside it' (BR 46). This is essentialist and performed identity intertwined; it is neither the silence of the repressed Slave, nor the voice of the powerful Master. And this is also a political treatment of race as both essentialist and constructed notion of diversity. On the contrary, the speaking voice is powerful precisely at the moment when she is separated from herself — 'each separate part without knowledge of the other separate parts' (BR 48). The blackness is compared to the silent voice by rejecting the binary logic of oppositional thinking; the silent voice 'stands opposite the blackness and yet it does not oppose the blackness, because conflict is not part of its nature' (BR 52). It is not imbued with hatred but rather with love, which brings down the boundaries of racism, colonialism and individual identity and introduces the complexity of the juxtaposition between the silent voice and the blackness: 'Living in the silent voice I am no longer 'I',' Jamaica Kincaid says in conclusion to this lyrical narrative, 'Living in the silent voice I am at last at peace. Living in the silent voice, I am at last erased' (BR 52). The conclusive words 'at last erased' are delivered to us with a triumphant tone which anticipates the final image of the novel Lucy in which the protagonist's empowered subjectivity is similarly figured as 'one great big blur' (L 164). To borrow from Gayatri Spivak, the silent voice could be defined as that which 'lingers in post-coloniality in the space of difference, in decolonized terrain.' As Spivak says of Mahasweta Devi, this is a space that cannot share in the reversal of the colonial logic as it is being adopted by the new, independent nation; on the contrary, it is 'the space of the displacement of the colonization-decolonization reversal . . . [which] can become . . . a representation of decolonization as such.'[12] To reiterate in terms of the company that joins Kincaid in my own readings, this 'silent voice' inhabiting the place of displacement echoes Angela Carter's concept of 'decolonialized language and thought' and expresses a subjectivity that is capable of speaking in the new language which Luce Irigaray deems necessary in order to avoid repeating the same story. In other words, her utterance is made of that very poetry which 'is not a luxury' that Audre Lorde so effectively demonstrated to be necessary for the subaltern to be able to speak, an act which is possible when the blackness is 'at last erased,' the dominating voice rejected, and the silent voice liberated in its definitionless complexity.

Equally open, fragmentary, multiple and paradoxical is also the 'frightening I' in the story 'Wingless.' It is at the same time 'unaware ... defenseless and pitiful' (*BR* 23), 'primitive and wingless,' and yet it has the strength to declare:

> I shall grow up to be a tall, graceful, and altogether beautiful woman, and I shall impose on large numbers of people my will and also, for my own amusement, great pain. But now I shall try to see clearly. I shall try to tell differences. (*BR* 22).

In the future — like the panoptic eye of the omniscient narrator in the logocentric tradition that can see from the God-like vantage point above the world — she 'shall impose' her 'will' and 'great pain.' Right away domination and prevarication over other people are dissociated from understanding; in a few sentences devastatingly exposing the fictionality of racial, sexual, and national separations among individuals, it is declared that she, on the contrary and 'now,' will 'try to see clearly ... try to tell differences.' MacDonald-Smythe rightly observes that the story shows how maternal authority functions as survival strategy to learn how to be able to accept fearful and mysterious facts of life.[13] The acknowledgement of the mother's tongue links the young protagonist not only to her mother but most importantly to her own oral culture and community and imbue Kincaid's autobiographical narratives with historiographic characteristics.

This questioning of the unity of the self reaches its climax towards the end of the collection:

> I stood as if I were a prism, many-sided and transparent, refracting and reflecting light as it reached me, light that never could be destroyed. And how beautiful I became. (*BR* 80)

This is made possible by setting the narrative in the maternal context that blurs the distinction between open and closed, between One and Other, like — Luce Irigaray would note — the lips of the female sex and the body of the pregnant woman. This is a world in which 'the sun and the moon shone at the same time' (*BR* 77).

The tremendous strength of Kincaid's stories lies in their capacity to resist all canons: they move at the beat of drums and the rhythm of jazz, so that we may be tempted to subsume them under the label of

Black Aesthetics.[14] Yet, sometimes the sound effect is more like that of a
nursery rhyme and the invitation is to consider them exemplary of
'feminine language,' the nurse's language of sounds and silence which
stands before and beyond the rational signifying words of the father.
This is the language of the mother and child in the story 'My Mother':
'My mother and I wordlessly made an arrangement — I sent out my
beautiful sighs; she received them' (BR 56).

All stories are structured around the figure of the mother: the writer
is constantly connecting artistic creativity to maternity in the effort to
relate a new representation of the feminine which includes the logic of
maternal love. The commitment to this new ethics moves in the direction
supported, among others, by Julia Kristeva and Luce Irigaray: bringing
the maternal into the discourse of the father represents the new voice
outside the dichotomy of sexual difference.

And again, under the influence of Henry Louis Gates's formulation
of 'signifying' as the main feature of Black Aesthetics, one could conclude
that At the Bottom of the River is a successful example of this Afro-American
rhetorical strategy.[15] Parody, repetition, and inversion mark every single
movement of Kincaid's narrative.

To add one more side to the 'prism' of the new self, one could note
the insistent refusal to stick to a definitive statement by going back to
the beginning again and again: open-ended postmodernist fiction, one
could conclude. For example, 'What I Have Been Doing Lately' ends
where it begins and it re-begins in the middle of its non-linear movement
(BR 43), and the ultimate order/meaning is never reached: 'On the sides
of the deep hole I could see things written, but perhaps it was in a foreign
language because I couldn't read them' (BR 42). And yet, as 'things written'
they are inscribed in our memory, open to what Toni Morrison calls re-
memorying, interpreting and retelling. Thus, although the narrator
'doesn't know anymore,' has 'no words' (BR 30), 'no name' for her identity
(BR 80), nevertheless she cries out her powerful 'no' against the existing
order of things: 'I said, I don't like this. I don't want to do this anymore'
(BR 45). She finds the strength to escape annihilation (BR 81) in a strong
and yet un-authoritative voice that concludes the whole collection:

> ... how bound up I know I am to all that is human endeavor, to all that
> is past and to all that shall be, to all that shall be lost and leave no trace.
> I claim these things then-mine-and now feel myself grow solid and
> complete, my name filling up my mouth. (BR 82)

It shouldn't come as much of a surprise that this paradoxical fiction was given such a rough ride by the first reviewers, puzzled and disturbed by its being 'almost insultingly obscure,' as Anne Tyler puts it, a position shared also by Edith Milton who judges 'Miss Kincaid's penchant for apocalyptic imagery disturbing,' and Suzanne Freeman who defines her writing as 'quirky enough to challenge our very definition of what a short story should be.'[16] Later this initial uneasiness was replaced by a myriad of appreciative critical readings.

In my own 1990 interpretation I insisted on the concept 'resistance postmodernism' to convey the rich negotiations among various discourses that Kincaid enacts in her stories. I still believe that this theoretical stance takes us farther than accounting for paradoxically coexisting narrative features and opens possibilities for 'rethinking thinking,' a commitment which is as imperative after the 9-11 trauma as it was in the 1980s. This Western Euro-centric perspective certainly needed to be integrated with — yet not replaced by — Caribbean-informed readings. There remains the interpretative challenge to avoid reducing Kincaid's silent voice to a-historical language playing, as well as to avoid turning her into a truthful native informant. Helen Pyne Timothy captured this ambivalence in 1990, when she underlined that the stories reflect the 'complex moral cosmology Caribbean girls must inhabit' as they leave the paradisal union with their mothers of their infancy to grow into women, to gain a European education in order to advance socially in a colonial context, and to learn survival strategies so as to situate themselves as Black women in a racist culture.[17] Alison Donnell, in 1993, was also respectful of Kincaid's composite perspective when she underlined her questioning of Caribbean womanhood from within the Caribbean tradition of childhood novels.[18] Lizabeth Paravisini-Gebert, in 1999, insisted on a feminist reading based on Nancy Chodorow to underline how *At the Bottom of the River* uses the figure of the mother to impose a colonial and patriarchal education upon the girl who, in turn, stands as 'representative of Antigua's attempts to nurture its own political and cultural independence.'[19] Isobel Hoving, in 2001, while discussing in details the perils of subsuming texts from 'contact zones' under mainstream labels such as postmodern and the eclectic model of the crossroads, privileges a thematic approach, emphasizing anger as Kincaid's main characteristic, and concluding nevertheless that this theme provides the stories' postcolonial grounding.[20]

Annie John (1985)[21]

Even though *Annie John* initially received a more favorable welcome than *At the Bottom of the River*, it is interesting to note how it divides reviewers who still are preoccupied with definitions of genre. For instance, John Bemrose labels it 'a collection,' Bruce Van Wyngarden takes it for granted that it is 'a novel,' while Patricia O'Connor calls it 'an autobiographical narrative.'[22] However, all seem to agree that its autobiographical character and the realistic descriptions of Antigua should take most of the credit for its success, and in 1999 Laura Niesen de Abruna declared *Annie John* Kincaid's 'best work to date.'[23] Nevertheless, simply because both the literary tradition and feminism have embraced autobiography as the 'official' women's genre, we shouldn't assume that Kincaid has not challenged the supposition that women's autobiographical writing follows a given, realistic model.

The Third Chapter of *Annie John* provides us with a clue to the author's interpretation of autobiographical writing. The personal essay written for class by the twelve year-old Annie can be taken as a metaphor of the entire autobiographical novel: it demonstrates that 'lies' must enter autobiography when this is meant for a public audience (*AJ* 45). This position will be taken to its extreme narrative consequences later in *The Autobiography of My Mother*, which, exactly like *Annie John*, focuses on Annie and her mother and opens with the description of a paradisal Lacanian Imaginary pre-Oedipal stage. The union between mother and child is given by the scene at the sea when the two swim together in a relation of total dependence in which the daughter enjoys 'all the sounds' of the world by placing her ear against her mother's neck as if it were a sea shell.

The second part of the girl's essay describes the Symbolic phase, with the mother on a rock 'tracing patterns' with the father; the water separates them from the desperate daughter. The story is then a metaphor of the Oedipal crisis with the father splitting up the dyadic unity between child and mother and the coming into existence of the speaking subject as a consequence of the desire for the lost mother. It is, in other words, the entrance into the Symbolic dominated by the Phallus which Annie cannot accept. Therefore, she imposes a fictional closure on her autobiographical essay: she has her mother shed tears and hold her, rather than simply speak, in order to soothe her anxiety. This 'lie' is a return to the repressed union of the 'old days,' a hiding of the 'bad' side of reality.

Autobiography, then, manages to give us a feminist voice that stresses personal experience over the authoritarian universal without, in so doing, resulting in a demand for realism over symbolism, nor posing the author as the transcendental signifier of the text, as its meaning and origin. The pre-Oedipal unity in which the selves of mother and daughter are undifferentiated is the paradise of the first two chapters of *Annie John*, before the 'young-lady business' (*AJ* 26):

> As she told me the stories, I sometimes sat at her side, or would crouch on my knees behind her back and lean over her shoulder. As I did this, I would occasionally sniff at her neck, or behind her ears, or at her hair. She smelled sometimes of lemons, sometimes of sage, sometimes of roses, sometimes of bay leaf. At times I would no longer hear what it was she was saying; I just liked to look at her mouth as it opened and closed over words, or as she laughed. (*AJ* 22)

The perfect relationship between mother and daughter, it should be underlined, entails an equal attention to the language of meaning and that of feeling, to the words of concepts and those of sounds — to poetry.

The narrative keeps interrogating this relationship, also after 'all this was finished' (*AJ* 32) and the realization that, despite the same name, the two of them are two separate selves: 'She was my mother, Annie; I was her daughter, Annie' (*AJ* 105). Even after the two are physically separated, and her mother has become 'just a dot in the matchbox-size launch swallowed up in the big blue sea' (*AJ* 148), the caring and nurturing mother is always present, travelling mysteriously across space and time. So mother Annie will keep her word, 'it doesn't matter what you do or where you go, I'll always be your mother and this will always be your home' (*AJ* 147) — mysteriously, like Ma Chess who comes and goes 'on a day when the steamer was not due in port' (*AJ* 127).

The duality and non-linear temporality of the maternal cannot be comprehended by the causal discourse of a linear logic. Luce Irigaray, in *Ethique de la différence sexuelle*, has noted that the concept of sexual difference rests on the interdependence between space and time, i.e., on the spatialization of time that Kincaid has dismantled in *A Small Place*. But, as Julia Kristeva in *Women's Time* has pointed out, the time of feminine subjectivity is either cyclical or monumental — the repetition of biological cycles and the myth of the archaic Mother — rather than linear and spatial.[24] For a re-definition of sexual difference outside the traditional dichotomy, it is necessary to reconcile these separate conceptions of time and to redefine the relationship time-space. This is what Kincaid's writing and thinking do. For example, it dismantles the trope that equates house to woman as the place that traditionally has been used to inscribe woman within the patriarchal social order, when Ma Chess says: 'A house? Why live in a house? All you need is a nice hole in the ground, so you can come and go as you please' (*AJ* 126). This short quotation is exemplary of Kincaid's capacity to contain in a single sentence — her capacity to think through the language of poetry — a whole articulation of a very complex concept. In fact, the answer to the question 'Why live in a house?' uproots the entire idea of historical progress to show that the move from the primitive condition of living in a 'hole' to the modern condition of living in a 'house' has entailed a confinement of women's freedom. Within the logic of gender division, woman is given a house within which walls she remains properly confined; thus Ma Chess's comment indicates a radical refusal of patriarchal order. It suggests that the liberation of the female subject passes through the rejection of the woman-house, an issue which is fundamental in the context of what Carole Davies has aptly called 'the overwhelming Caribbean culture of the household.'[25] In her essay, which also provides a stimulating reading of *Annie John* and *At the Bottom of the River*, Davies rightly considers the house — the place of the mother and female lineage — as the locus for self-definition and points out how revisitations of such places are a necessary step for the definition of the Caribbean female self. For reasons linked to emigration, these revisitations often occur only in writing.

In addition and still with regard to the redefinition of the concept space-time, *Annie John* plays with realistic objective temporality: the adverbial phrase 'On the Sunday before the Monday' (*AJ* 29) is the most visible example of the mocking of spatialized temporality operating within a narrative that never refers to a time outside that of its own story. There are no dates in this autobiographical novel, but only the age of the protagonist: rather than a universal interpretation of history, we have a 'conversation piece':

> The rain went on in this way for over three months. By the end of it, the sea had risen and what used to be dry land was covered with water and crabs lived there. In spite of what everyone said, the sea never did go back to the way it had been, and what a great conversation piece it

made to try and remember what used to be there where the sea now stretched up to. (*AJ* 109)

Together with the dismantling of the sexual polarization, *Annie John* deconstructs also the dichotomy Master-Slave that is at the foundation of the colonial enterprise, resulting in a powerful cry of protest. After mocking the English for their questionable personal cleanliness ('Have you ever noticed how they smell as if they had been bottled up in a fish?' [*AJ* 36]), after having the English girl wear the dunce cap in class, and after stressing that 'our ancestors' — the 'slaves' — 'had done nothing wrong except sit somewhere, defenseless,' she refuses to appropriate the Western concept of national and personal identity to express her anger at colonialism. Rather, she dismantles the very dialectics that supports it and notes:

> Of course, sometimes, what with our teachers and our books, it was hard for us to tell on which side we really now belonged — with the masters or the slaves — for it was all history, it was all in the past, and everybody behaved differently now....

She says so, adding with revolutionary anti-colonial pathos:

> ... if the tables had been turned we would have acted differently; I was sure that if our ancestors had gone from Africa to Europe and come upon the people living there, they would have taken a proper interest in the Europeans on first seeing them, and said, 'How nice,' and then gone home to tell their friends about it. (*AJ* 76)

This conclusion will be echoed later in *A Small Place*. It provides a further example to support the comparison of Kincaid's discourse with Spivak's. The position occupied by the subaltern voice of Mahasweta — the only voice which can really speak for decolonization, since it is situated beyond and outside the binary opposition empire-colony — is similar to that occupied by Annie John. It is worth recalling that the quotation above is placed in the memorable chapter 'Columbus in Chains,' where under a picture of an imprisoned Christopher Columbus, Annie prints in Old English lettering: 'The Great Old Man Can No Longer Just Get Up and Go' (*AJ* 78). The passage could find its explanation in the essay where the Native tells the Foreigner: 'there must have been some good people among you, but they stayed home. And that is the point. That is why they are good. They stayed home' (SP 35).

The episode of Columbus recalls the fundamental role played by the educational system within a colonized situation. This function is stressed in A Small Place in relation to the discussion of the Old Library and the New Library, this being a building under repair since 1974. The library here serves as a perfect metaphor for colonial as well as post-/neo-colonial conditions: the Old Library — from which the narrator 'stole many books' (SP 45) — contained 'the fairy tale of how we met you, your right to do the things you did, how beautiful you were, are, and always will be' (SP 42), whereas the New Library does not exist yet — a perfect symbol of the devastation which exists for a people deprived of their own culture. It symbolizes a state that needs also a Minister of Culture — a need explicitly condemned by Kincaid through her comment: 'in places where there is a Minister of Culture it means there is no culture.' These places must be like 'Countries with Liberty Weekend' (SP 49), she continues, clearly relating Antigua's neo-colonial misery to US imperialism, which is perpetrated in the name of liberty but entails the systematic violation of liberty.

Grounded on personal experience, Kincaid's writing nonetheless defies a realistic interpretation of her voice; it challenges any possibility of deciphering a single meaning by emphasizing multiplicity in what Roland Barthes has called 'an anti-theological activity,' which is 'truly revolutionary since to refuse to fix meaning is, in the end, to refuse God and his hypostases — reason, science, law.'[26] It is in an anti-teleological narrative that Kincaid keeps engaging a devastating critique of Colonialism and Patriarchy in the forms they have assumed in the contemporary power system. To the tourists in Antigua, Kincaid's books may provide the right lenses to see what is at the bottom of the Caribbean Sea: not only the contents of the lavatories which the developers of today have failed to connect to a proper sewage-system, but also the 'large number of black slaves' whom the past exploiters have kidnapped across the ocean (SP 14). To the readers of Annie John, Kincaid offers a Bildungsroman in which gender and racial constructs are integral parts of knowledge formation. Evelyn O'Callaghan aptly captures this complexity when in her analysis of the novel, she convincingly shows that:

Annie John demonstrates the construction of colonial woman within imperial and patriarchal discourse, and disrupts the hegemony of such discourse by questioning its assumptions, particularly ... [by] refusing the idea that women's sexuality is rooted in sin and results in death .... *Annie John* suggests that acquiescing in patriarchy ... results in death of female subjectivity and agency.

Additionally ... the novel conflates female Othering with colonial Othering. In appropriating myths that construct woman/native in certain pejorative ways, the post-colonial feminist text regains some measure of control over them; in querying their construction it undermines their ideological power. Finally by locating themselves in the specifically West Indian context, such texts demonstrate how contending discourses ... problematize women's self-definitions in the region.'[27]

Lucy (1990)[28]

Kincaid pursues her devastating critique of colonialism and patriarchy in a language so new that the whole history of colonialism undergoes a radical revision. Kenneth Ramchad has pointedly discussed the following passage in Kincaid's *At the Bottom of the River* as exemplary of her 'literary orality':[29]

I leaf through the book, looking only at the pictures, which are bright and beautiful. From my looking through the book the word 'thorax' sticks in my mind. 'Thorax,' I say, 'thorax, thorax,' I don't know how many times... Oh sensation. I am filled with sensation. I feel-oh, how I feel. I feel, I feel, I feel. I have no words right now for how I feel. (*BR* 29-30)

I would suggest this passage is analogous to the following scene in *Lucy*, a text which was critically praised as an autobiographical *Kunslerroman*:

'... Let's go feed the minions.' [said Mariah]
It's possible that what she really said was 'millions,' not 'minions.' Certainly she said it in jest. But as we were cooking the fish, I was thinking about it. 'Minions.' A word like that would haunt someone like me; the place where I came from was a dominion of someplace else. I became so taken with the word 'dominion'... (*L* 37)

The insistent focus on signifiers throughout invites me to play with the title word 'Lucy.' Lucy as she who brings light/enlightenment, insight; as the brightest morning star Venus, which also stands for sexual desire; as female Lucifer — and this is in the title story — the proud, rebellious archangel, Satan; Lucy also as the female skeleton of the hominid found in Ethiopia in 1974 and named after the Beatles' song 'Lucy in the Sky with Diamonds'; finally, Lucy as a Lucy Stoner advocating the retention of maiden names through marriage, or as a Lucy Terry, North America's first Black poet.

But who is Lucy in the book Lucy? 'Lucy is the only character drawn directly from life,' declares Kincaid in an interview, allowing the equation of the character's name Lucy Josephine Potter with her own real name, Elaine Cynthia Potter Richardson.[30] Also, Lucy is the protagonist of the five stories which read as the continuation/repetition of the life of the nameless speaking-I in *At the Bottom of the River* and of Annie in *Annie John*. The title itself already draws our attention to the fact that things are more simple and yet more complicated than a mere choice between either fiction or autobiography. The specification that continues Kincaid's declaration about *Lucy* points towards such complexity by a masterful ironic use of the double negative: 'but I would never say I wouldn't write about an experience I've had.'[31]

That a simple title like *Lucy* triggers such an intricate network of interpretations should not surprise. Throughout Kincaid's work, the use of language is deceptively straightforward, as in the declaration above about the autobiographical nature of her novel. The transparency of her primitive, child-like voice exposes the elaborate politics at the core of her writings, making us soon realize that her texts function as palimpsests. The artless simplicity of her oral syntax is delusive: irony as well as lexical and phonetic repetitions chain her sentences together into a literary composition that engages in an endless movement between sameness and difference, beyond both fixed identity and heterogeneous indifferent fluidity — a movement back-and-forth that keeps difference always already significant by anchoring its identity on the historical temporality of being-in-the-world. Not surprisingly and like Kincaid's previous and ·subsequent works, *Lucy* poses a problem of genre definition. The attraction of Lucy lies in the foregrounding of the definition of an identity which is posed in terms of survival strategy — an oxymoronic identity/ dis-identity which transcends the polarity Sameness-Difference and which already finds expression in the eloquent 'silent voice' of the nameless prismatic 'I' in *At the Bottom of the River*. When placed within the rhetorical and structural frame of autobiography, this postmodern, open, fragmentary, multiple and paradoxical subjectivity — a decolonialized subjectivity — precipitates the self-consciousness of the woman's place both as the cultural construct 'woman' and as author. As Sidonie Smith states in her seminal study *A Poetics of Women's Autobiography*, 'autobiography' no longer makes sense culturally' because new ideologies of selfhood have fractured its form and 'women writing autobiography in the twentieth century explore alternative scenarios of textuality and sexuality,' disrupting the notions of author and woman alike.[32]

I like to think of the 'alternative scenario' explored by Lucy as a quilted autobiographical narrative, with the five stories forming the volume being the larger pieces of material forming the central pattern. As such, they demand to be viewed closely, in order to examine the fine work of their stitches, and also from afar, to capture the total effect of the quilt. This metaphor suggests that a linear reading will be unproductive, despite the ordered chronological development of the events which bring the protagonist to her economic and artistic independence.

The five stories stretch exactly over the period of one year, beginning with 'Poor Visitor' and the narrator's first day in her new place (unnamed, but seemingly New York), where it is as cold 'as it was expected to be in the middle of January' (*L* 3); then the speaking-I experiences her first spring in the story 'Mariah' and her first summer vacation by one of the Great Lakes in 'The Tongue,' after which she returns to the city in October where the story 'Cold Heart' begins; finally, she takes us back to January — 'a new beginning again' (*L* 133) — in the opening scene of the last piece, the title-story. The seasonal cycle also functions as the sound-track of the plot. This takes the protagonist from a village in the West Indies to a city in the US, in a geographical movement from the colonies to the core of the present empire, as well as in a psychological movement towards her hatred for the new place growing to match her hatred for the home she has left behind. It is a movement from opposition to sameness within difference characterizing the two opposite worlds. In the end, spatial and emotional movements merge to express and to accept the oxymoron of postcoloniality, which blurs while it magnifies the difference between the so-called Third and First Worlds.

During the passing of the four seasons, Lucy decides that being an au pair still means living with a family, defined alternatively as 'the millstone around your life's neck' (L 8), or the locus of 'untruths that I had only just begun to see as universal' (L 77), and by the end of the year she moves into a rented apartment and finds a secretarial job. In the process, she learns to appreciate her mother's principle that 'Everything remains the same and yet nothing is the same' (L 78) — a principle which governs the structural, rhetorical and thematic organization of her discourse throughout Lucy. 'Everything remains the same,' as the flowered material of the small pieces forming the quilt, because January is just as cold and unpleasant in the first piece as it is in the last a year later, and because the conflictual relationship between mother and daughter is expressed in both episodes through letters 'full of lies.' Yet, 'nothing is the same' too, because if we look closely we can see that the flowers in each patch have slightly different colours and the fact that Lucy leaves Mariah's family brings a whole set of different colours to her own life.

One significant difference which is also a sameness is Lucy's attitude towards her own name. She is nameless until the last story, but the final act of naming herself in the piece 'Lucy' does not entail any more knowledge of herself: 'The person I had become I did not know very well' (L 133), she states in unquestionable terms. In 'Poor Visitor' she refers to herself merely as a 'young girl' with 'brown' skin and eyes, adding that her host family calls her 'the Visitor,' and declaring, 'I was very unhappy' (L 9). Otherwise, she only defines herself in negative clauses, as in the following examples: 'something I had always known [her race and name] . . . was not so. I was no longer in a tropical zone' (L 5) and 'I was not cargo. . . I was not even the maid' (L 7). Emblematic of her choice of utterances which must affirm their subject in order to negate it is the recurrence of the word 'untruth,' in lieu of 'lie,' 'fiction', 'story', or 'invention', as if a veiled/masked truth were less real or less faithful than a falsehood. Her self-definition through the sameness/difference of the negative clause continues and gains full significance in the next story, 'Mariah', where Lucy explores the ways in which she is different from the mother of her host family — somebody 'beyond doubt or confidence', since 'the thing she wants to happen happens' (L 26) to her. Mariah can best be captured in the last, irresistible scene of the story:

... she turned and said 'I was looking forward to telling you that I have Indian blood.... But now, I don't know why, I feel I shouldn't tell you that. I feel you will take it the wrong way.'

This really surprised me. What way should I take this? Wrong way? Right way? What could she mean? To look at her, there was nothing remotely like an Indian about her. Why claim a thing like that? I myself had Indian blood in me. My grandmother is a Carib Indian. That makes me one quarter Carib Indian. But I don't go around saying that I have Indian blood in me. The Carib Indians were good sailors, but I don't like to be on the sea; I only like to look at it. To me my grandmother is my grandmother, not an Indian. My grandmother is alive; the Indians she came from are all dead. If someone could get away with it, I am sure they would put my grandmother in a museum....

Mariah says, 'I have Indian blood in me, 'and underneath everything I could swear she says as if she were announcing her possession of a trophy. How do you get to be the sort of victor who can claim to be the vanquished also? (L 39-41)

The comparison with Mariah is emblematic of a positing of her identity in relational terms. Lucy's question is never 'Who am I?' but always 'Who am I in relation to an Other?' Crucial in this regard and relevant to 'the Woman question' is the confrontation of the speaking subject with the mother, both her actual mother and the mother-figure Mariah. Moreover, the passage is also a clear example of the I-Thou mode of narrative, fully explored in *A Small Place*, which rhetorically multiplies the possibilities of meaning by inviting the reader to participate. Finally, this scene brings to the foreground the tissue of repetitions that constitute Kincaid's prose. The dilemma directed at the reader — 'How does a person get to be that way?' — appears with the insistence of a refrain in Lucy, with its numerous variants accounting for the direct construction of the personalities of Mariah, Dinah, the mother and Lucy.

The focus on Mariah, who is an American liberal feminist, elicits a comparison with Lucy's mother, a Black housewife in the West Indies, so that two apparently different types of women merge into sameness:

Mariah wanted all of us, the children and me, to see things the way she did.... But I already had a mother who loved me, and I had come to see her love as a burden. ... I had come to feel that my mother's love for me was designed solely to make me into an echo of her. ... I felt that I would rather be dead than become just an echo of someone. (L 35-36)

Lucy clearly emerges as a prismatic subjectivity who wants to relate to others but not mirror them: she is not looking for a model; rather she is looking for a context in which her relational subjectivity can become agency.

In 'The Tongue,' Mariah continues to be a negative model for the still nameless young girl. Nevertheless, here Lucy repeats how much she likes her, shifting her self-definition from rejection to acceptance of differences. This is an important step towards her confrontation with her mother, fully explored in the following section. Conversely, 'Cold Heart' starts out with an acceptance of the past:

> I could see the sameness in everything; I could see the present take a shape — the shape of my past.
> My past was my mother.... I was not like my mother — I was my mother. (L 90)

And yet, this recognition does not prevent her from stating a little later, 'I am not like my mother' (L 123), when her resemblance is pointed out by the much despised cousin Maude. The contradiction is made even more explicit in the final words of the story, where she refers to her trauma at the birth of the first of her three brothers when the unconditional love of her mother was taken away from her forever: '... for ten of my twenty years, half of my life, I had been mourning the end of a love affair, perhaps the only true love in my whole life I would ever know ...' (L 132). This conclusion makes absolutely clear that the complications she struggles against in defining herself are associated with her unresolved problematic relationship with her mother. Thus the meaning Lorna Goodison gives to the line 'I am becoming my mother' is the same which we are supposed to give to Kincaid's apparently contradictory statements: Lucy is in the process, indeed, of birthing herself, becoming her own empowered individual, capable of temporary self-definitions and of contextual identifications, as she passes through life.

It is in the story 'Lucy' that the focus on the autobiographical voice is sharpened — namely, where Lucy declares: 'I understood that I was inventing myself . . .' (L 134). This statement clearly challenges the notion of referentiality and authenticity of the self, shattering a milestone of traditional notions of autobiography and identity. Placed within a context that articulates a conflictual mother-daughter relationship, this sentence exemplifies what Smith has called 'a poetics of women's autobiography.' Lucy is a female autobiographer who 'traces her origins to and through, rather than against, the mother whose presence has been repressed in order for the symbolic contract to emerge.'[33] She has now rejected the models of her own mother and of Mariah, and she is getting ready for 'a new beginning.' However, her task will always be rooted in her origin and will always be difficult, as the following reflection shows:

> I was born on an island.... I know this: it was discovered by Christopher Columbus in 1493; Columbus never set foot there but only named it in passing, after a church in Spain. He could not have known that he would have so many things to name, and I imagined how hard he had to rack his brain after he ran out of names honoring his benefactors, the saints he cherished, events important to him. A task like that would have killed a thoughtful person, but he went on to live a very long life. (*L* 134-135)

Because she, on the contrary, is a very thoughtful person, she finds it very hard to find a name even for herself, let alone for the whole of the 'new world'!

And it is again because she is a very thoughtful person that her self-invention culminates in the acceptance of the name that is printed on her documents and was given to her by her mother. This is so, despite the recognition that 'your past is the person you no longer are, the situations you are no longer in' (*L* 137). At this point Lucy has learned from photography that language and reality are not interchangeable, and thus that identity cannot be either essentialist or nominalist but rather an articulation of both: 'I would try and try to make a print that made more beautiful the thing I thought I had seen, that would reveal to me some of the things I had not seen, but I did not succeed' (*L* 160). So she finally declares she is Lucy Josephine Potter, even though she admits that she 'used to hate all three of those names' (*L* 149) — Potter, because it belonged to the Englishmen who owned her ancestors when they were slaves; Josephine, because it came from an uncle who was supposed to leave some money for her in his will but lost it all; and Lucy because 'it seemed slight, without substance' (*L* 149).

Potter reflects the history of her race and nation, and Josephine that of her class and family. Yet again, what about Lucy? Lucy certainly gains a powerful substance in these pages. Lucy first tells us she 'felt like Lucifer, doomed to build wrong upon wrong' in a furious rejection of Mariah's suggestion that she may feel guilty after her father's death (*L* 139). And after she has revealed and explained her three names, Lucy remembers her mother's reply when she asked the reasons for naming her so: 'I named you after Satan himself. Lucy, short for Lucifer. What a botheration from the moment you were conceived' (*L* 152). To which the daughter reacts:

> I was transformed from failure to triumph.... Lucy, a girl's name for Lucifer. That my mother would have found me devil-like did not surprise me, for I often thought of her as god-like, and are not the children of gods devils? I did not grow to like the name Lucy — I would have much preferred to be called Lucifer outright — but whenever I saw my name I always reached out to give it a strong embrace. (*L* 152-153)

Lucy embraces her slight/powerful, inherited/invented full name in the final scene where 'everything remains the same and nothing is the same' and empowers herself to the point of being able to act upon the world:

> I wrote my full name: Lucy Josephine Potter. At the sight of it many thoughts rushed through me, but I could write down only this: 'I wish I could love someone so much that I could die from it.' And then as I looked at this sentence a great wave of shame came over me and I wept and wept so much that the tears fell on the page and caused all the words to become one great big blur. (*L* 162-63)

Not only because Kincaid's autobiography is told in the form of five stories, but also because it focuses the self-definition of the speaking subject on the problematic issue concerning the communication between mother and daughter, the articulation of a relationship which patriarchy has not named in its right terms yet, it shows that identity is an 'invention,' a creative activity that is always in progress because subjectivity is never fixed. Despite its linguistic origin, such creation provides a fundamental grounding for experience and social agency. I thereby read this fluid identity in Kincaid's truthful fictions in the terms she uses to describe the process of her own writing:

It's just like walking ... on empty space. Every step you take you have
to build something under it. Sometimes it would take me days to build
up a sentence, and I would have to come back because it had gone too
far. I was always somewhat frightened... I had points of reality that I
had to have... [34]

Similarly, identity is that 'something' we build in order to walk along
— the necessary scaffolding for constructing a house — but in the case
of *Lucy*, the scaffolding is still there, a sort of Pompidou Centre which
addresses directly and visibly the question of female subjectivity, and in
so doing undermines the very humanistic foundation of the androcentric
contract of autobiography as the history of the Self. Following the
indication of Smith, especially in her interpretation of Maxine Hong
Kingston's The *Woman Warrior*, I read *Lucy* as part of the postcolonial
revision of the tradition established by Gertrude Stein's *The Autobiography
of Alice B. Toklas* and *Everybody's Autobiography*. Lucy reads as five
confrontations with the fiction of self-representation and with the
autobiographical possibilities embedded in the cultural fiction of gender
roles; each book is composed of five stories which have fractured formal
autobiographies beyond recognition; in addition, each work expresses
the complications of mother-daughter relations within patriarchal culture.
Similarly to Kingston's novel, a cyclical movement characterizes Kincaid's
text, an apparent line of progress that in the end returns to the beginning.
In addition, both are rooted in the working class and the ethnic margins
of American culture, thus bringing to the autobiographical project
complicating perspectives on the relationship of woman to language and
to narrative, and embracing a definition of the gendered subject in all its
complex relation to a symbolic order subjected to a radical postcolonial
revision. Moira Ferguson unquestionably and convincingly considers *Lucy*
exemplary of 'the process of self-decolonization.'[35]
     With its publication in 1990, the gendered subject Lucy brought
an important contribution to the debate among feminist theorists on the
related concepts of *woman* and *gender*. She showed that an identity can
actually be asserted and denied at the same time, and that the oxymoron
of the woman speaking within, while existing only outside the Symbolic,
can in fact be accepted as politically significant. In *Lucy* we find a
consciousness such as that theorized by Linda Alcoff in terms of 'a
positionality within a context,' or a speaking subject which Teresa de
Lauretis defined as 'a dynamic process,' semiotically constructed through

practice and experience; Lucy is what Spivak called 'a questioning subject' committed to essentialism but only 'strategically,' or what Trinh Minh-ha declared to 'baffle definition,' because gender is 'a social regulator as well as a political potential for change.'[36] Lucy's self is imbued but not overdetermined by race, gender, class, and nationality. Her subjectivity is always already de-essentialized, and yet defined by the assumption of a definite positionality within different contexts. Lucy's identity is the strategic consciousness kept in fluid interaction and constant motion by a practice of self-analysis. Lucy's self is relational to a moving context and yet also a locus for the construction of meaning — an example of how feminist theory and practice can avoid the impasse imposed by the obligatory choice between either the essentialism of liberal and cultural feminists' conceptions of *woman* as a biologically grounded subject, or the nominalism of poststructural feminists' rejection of the concept *woman* as semiotic discourse. It is precisely because she both rejects Mariah's essentialist explanations and accepts to name and write herself that Lucy shows how the polarized terms of this controversy can be made to coexist. Lucy embraces what has all too often and too simply been stigmatized as the double bind of feminism, namely, that its existence is justified only by the existence of women's submission and alienation, which is precisely what feminism is meant to expose as a delusory imposition upon reality. Kincaid's discourse proves it is not necessary to exclude in order to affirm: Lucy can be 'other' and yet at times 'love' Mariah as well as hate her mother. Just as her mother and Mariah are always present in Lucy's struggle for self-affirmation, so 'the other woman' is never forgotten in this text, which follows Jane Gallop's forcible recommendation to hold onto 'the rifts in feminist plenitude' in order to avoid the danger of effacing the differences among women.[37]

Lucy repeats that her life cannot be explained by the books which Mariah treasures (*L* 131-2, 142, 163), and the emphasis with which she differentiates herself from 'women in general' is parallel to that by which she rejects her own mother who — by marrying a man who left her in debt and by having had children — 'had betrayed herself' and 'her own intelligence' (*L* 127, 123). Neither the American 'liberated feminist' nor the Antiguan 'oppressed housewife' can provide her with a suitable model of identity. And yet, the alternative is not that of a dissolution of consciousness into the undifferentiated self of pure signifiers. The name she 'invents' for herself is nothing other than the name she was given at birth — a choice that grounds her identity in the temporally mutable but inerasable occasions of history.

The next question is, in what voice does Lucy speak? She speaks in contrapuntal fashion and precipitates both representation and self-representation. Although she declares that the Brontës are 'the authoresses whose books I loved' (L 149), and although she states that the 'invention' of herself is 'performed more in the way of a painter than in the way of a scientist' (L 134), Lucy doesn't think of herself as an artist. And yet the contrary is also true, because this indeed is a portrait of an artist, as Kincaid explicitly tells us: 'This is not about race and class. This is a person figuring out how to be an artist, an artist of herself and of things.'[38] Similarly to the existing category of *woman*, the term *artist* does not offer her a desirable identity:

> [T]hey seemed to take for granted that everything they said mattered. They were artists. I had heard of people in this position. I had never seen an example in the place where I came from. I noticed that mostly they were men. It seemed to be a position that allowed for irresponsibility.... Yes, I had heard of these people: they died insane, they died paupers, no one much liked them except other people like themselves. And I thought of all the people in the world I had known who went insane and died, and who drank too much rum and then died, and who were paupers and died, and I wondered if there were any artists among them. Who would have known? And I thought, I am not an artist, but I shall always like to be with the people who stand apart. (L 98)

Lucy is not an artist — once again the double talk of the negative clause — because she does not fit in the model provided by Western bourgeois culture. Lucy is not 'the excluded' who feels rejected by modernity's economic values in the various personae of the romantic, modernist, and avant-gardist artist, and yet she likes 'to stand apart'; all the artists of modernity express their desire, commitment, or dream to transform the existing world by situating themselves in oppositional autonomous terms vis-à-vis society, and in so doing providing a liberating ground for art.[39] It is this willed separateness, I suggest, that makes Lucy remark that she does not belong, despite her liking to be apart. In these terms, on the contrary, Lucy is an artist: she creates her own discourse, speaking in a voice under erasure that does dissolve her own identity 'in a big blur' but never without presenting it first as a clear picture: 'Lucy Josephine Potter.' Again, here is how Kincaid puts it: 'I'm trying to discover the secret of myself. If that's connected to the universe, I'm very grateful. But for me everything passes through the self.' This is how she has figured out 'how to be an artist, an artist of herself and of things.'[40] Helen Tiffin forcefully describes Lucy's artistic empowerment as a corporeal act that defies the reproduction of the already inscribed, when she interprets the description of Lucy's writing of her name being turned into a 'great big blur' by her own tears, with the following statement: 'Lucy's body has erased a final act of scriptorial obedience.'[41]

Kincaid's writing is neither the teleological variety of the androcentric, linear and unitary self constructed for and by the genre 'autobiography' nor is it the tangles, cuts and silences theorized by Kristeva as the writing of the maternal.[42] Lucy moves a step beyond Annie for whom the longed-for pre-Oedipal unity of the undifferentiated selves of mother and daughter is predominant. By bringing the maternal into the Symbolic, the discourse of the father, by showing that identity, once posited, is unbearable and must be continuously blurred, Lucy speaks from and to a place situated beyond the dichotomy of gender opposition. This does not mean that she speaks in a mythic androgynous voice. Lucy is a sexualized subjectivity in the same way as she is an artist, with a difference: she is a gendered subject who situates herself beyond gender binarism. She is also a postmodernist subject with a difference: Lucy continually moves between the claiming of truth and the deconstruction of truth; she forces us into a space that attacks the 'various versions of autonomy and integrity' that have so far characterized the relation between culture and society to focus instead, as McGowan puts it, 'on the alternative strategies for social action that postmodernism proposes as appropriate responses to foundationalism's demise and as adequate protections against the static social orders that have arisen in foundationalism's stead.'[43]

Similarly, by bringing the colonies to the metropolitan centre of the empire, by showing the displacement of the master-slave reversal, Lucy speaks also beyond the colonization-decolonization binarism. Lucy's voice comes to occupy a space that Shakespeare could not conceive, even in terms of desire. In *The Tempest* there is only one woman, Miranda, who becomes the signifier of *the Woman*, the monolithic entity *women in general* that triumphs in Mariah's books. Sycorax is left off stage and Caliban is allowed to long for and dream of only Miranda. Even Mary Wollstonecraft Shelley could not go farther than confining a voice like Lucy's to the space of unattainable desire. In fact, within the context of *Frankenstein*, Lucy speaks for that 'equal companion' whom the Monster so much longed for and Dr. Frankenstein destroyed right after having created. Lucy is a female Caliban, a monstrous creature whose identity shakes the boundaries between subject and object, by continuously challenging the boundaries of its own narrative. And yet, in Kincaid's texts she does speak her identity in order to break the long silence into which she has been confined.

Her voice is 'monstrous' because it combines elements which a binary order would keep separate; the Grenadian-American poet Audre Lorde expresses the present condition of this female Caliban speaking from her own 'monstrous' condition as a lesbian, a mother, and a woman of colour, in the following terms:

> ... living in the European mode, ... we rely solely upon ideas to make us free. . . .
>
> But as we come into touch with our ancient, non-european consciousness ... we learn more and more to cherish our feelings and to respect those hidden sources of our power from where true knowledge and, therefore, lasting action comes.
>
> ... the possibility for fusion of these two approaches [is] so necessary for our survival, and we come closest to this combination in our poetry. ...
>
> For women, then, poetry is not a luxury.[44]

Indeed Kincaid's poetry shows the need — not the luxury — of bringing together what Lucy calls the 'good idea' of New York (*L* 4) with the 'bad feelings' associated with Antigua (*L* 3) to create a fusion which brings her 'to love the idea of seasons,' as they 'give the earth a character with many personalities' (*L* 51-52). Multiplicity and change characterize Lucy with the same flexibility and determination as the seasons do in the temperate zones of the world.

She constantly warns us against grounding her discourse upon any presumed external foundation, and the passage in which she rejects a Freudian interpretation of her dreams is eloquent in this regard. The conclusion of 'Poor Visitor' makes clear that Western culture is not adequate to understand her. When she relates her dream of being chased by Mariah's husband and falling down a hole filled with blue and silver snakes, she expresses her bafflement at her host-family's reaction and their ignorance of her traditions:

> I did not know who Dr. Freud was. Then they laughed in a soft, kind way. I had meant by telling them my dream that I had taken them in, because only people who were very important to me had ever shown up in my dreams. I did not know if they understood that. (*L* 15)

With this straightforward rejection of the need for the external grounding characteristic of humanism, the first story sets the pace for the whole text, inviting us to turn the presumed ground of human experience into an object of anxious interrogation, like the signifier itself. This way Lucy's dreams enter the outside world to fuse with it in 'a great big blur' — a condition of being inside and outside — linked to the movement in and out of gender as ideological representation proposed by Teresa de Lauretis as characteristic of the subject of feminism.[45] Like the tapestries in Remedios Varo's paintings, Lucy's voice is in and out; it stands for God as well as for Satan, but also always it already stands for 'a slight' signifier, 'without substance,' thus providing a most effective example of the fundamental postmodern subsumption of signifiers back into the system of meaning and allowing through a provisional, relational 'prismatic identity' for the decolonialized subjectivity to be heard and defined not once and for all, not in the fixed way of an epic of arrival, but rather as the voice of errancy of a subject capable of continuously birthing herself and content to live on the run.

Lucy's is not a simplistic story of migration; Lucy complicates this story of upward mobility by articulating negotiations that are not only socio-economic but also artistic and emotional. In gaining economic independence through migration to the US, Lucy does not stop loving her own mother in favor of Mariah;[46] she does not join the community of metropolitan New York artists in order to reject Antigua's culture; rather, she 'claims the right/responsibility of loving denied to the subject that wishes to choose agency from victimage.'[47] Lucy expresses contemporary complexity through her dream in which she 'takes in' Mariah's family also because she thematizes the implications of a Third World woman's rise to independent agency, which is not devoid of risks of alliance with Western political, cultural, and affectionate constituencies.[48] Lucy takes this risk because she refuses to accept the established order of things. Audre Lorde would say that Lucy refuses the white fathers' dictum 'I think, therefore, I am' to embrace instead the whisper in our dreams of the black mother, 'I feel, therefore, I can be free.' Lorde suggests it is poetry which 'coins the language to express and chart [her] revolutionary demand'. As Lucy, alone in the foreign country, inundates her written expression of love ('I wish I could love someone so much that I could die') with her tears to form 'a great big blur' she is coining 'the language to express and chart her revolutionary demand' for a world undivided between the imperial centre and the colonial periphery.[49]

Notes

1   See Sidonie Smith, *A Poetics of Women's Autobiography: Marginality and the Fictions of Self-Representation*, Bloomington: Indiana University Press, 1987.
2   See Lorna Goodison, *I Am Becoming My Mother*, London: New Beacon, 1986.
3   See Gayatri C. Spivak, *In Other Worlds: Essays in Cultural Politics*, New York: Methuen, 1987.
4   See Toni Morrison, *Playing in the Dark: Whiteness and the Literary Imagination*, Cambridge: Harvard University Press, 1992.
5   See Adrienne Rich, *What is Found There, Notebooks on Poetry and Politics*, New York: Norton, 1993.
6   See Rosi Braidotti, *Nomadic Subjects*, New York: Columbia UP, 1994See Liana Borghi, 'Introduzione: L'occhio del[l]'ago' in Passaggi: *Letterature comparate al femminile*, Urbino: Quattroventi, 2002.
7   Feminist definitions of transnationality are deeply indebted to Adrienne Rich's 'Notes Towards a Politics of Location' in *Blood, Bread and Poetry: Selected Prose*, 1979-1985, New York: Norton, 1986: 210-2, p. 32. See Rosi Braidotti, *Metamorphoses: Towards a Materialist Theory of Becoming*, Cambridge: Polity, 2002.
8   Jessica Hagedorn, 'Crimson Prey for Audre Lorde' in *Terra Nova*, Washington, 1989.
9   Antonia MacDonald-Smythe, *Making Homes in the West Indies: Constructions of Subjectivity in the Writings of Michelle Cliff and Jamaica Kincaid*, New York: Garland, 2001, argues that Kincaid has made herself at home both in West Indian and North American literary space by claiming as home the various locations of herself as traveling subject. While I agree with MacDonald-Smythe's emphasis on Kincaid's transnational location, I am reluctant to subscribe to her interpretation that both the mother and Antigua — her family and her community — are frozen into a static vision of a past which Kincaid has abandoned when she went into exile. I also prefer to avoid using the expression exile, which recalls a modernist condition of cosmopolitan artists and writers; on the contrary, I think Kincaid's personal history of migration and her elaboration of a transnational cultural discourse share Lucy's need to differentiate herself from 'the artists' in New York (see discussion below).

10   An earlier version of this section was published as Giovanna Covi, 'Jamaica Kincaid and the Resistance to Canons,' in Carole Boyce Davies and Elaine Savory Fido, eds., *Out of the Kumbla: Caribbean Women and Literature*, Trenton: Africa World Press, 1990: 345-354.

11   Lizabeth Paravisini-Gebert, *Jamaica Kincaid: A Critical Companion*, Westport, CT: Greenwood Press, 1999. Paravisini-Gebert maintains that in 'Girl' 'we see the mother functioning as ... an agent of colonial assimilation, teaching her daughter ... behavior necessary to 'whiten' herself. ... the daughter's resistance stresses her preference for native ways and an affirmation of the native culture' (pp. 82-3). I would push this interpretation farther and say that the girl's 'silent voice' is postcolonial rather than anti-colonial, hence the complex relationship between Kincaid and her mother that is variously articulated in her works, underlining that storytelling is originated by the mother's tale but also that this tale can take infinite turns. For example, the juxtaposition between Girl as well as between adolescent Annie John and her mother is evident, but likewise is also evident the ambivalent relationship/identification between adult Xuela and her mother.

12   Gayatri C. Spivak, 'Woman in Difference' in Ross et al, eds., *Nationalism and Sexualities*, New York: Routledge, 1991:96-117, p. 97.

13   Antonia MacDonald-Smythe, *Making Homes in the West Indies*, p. 118.

14   See, for example, Amiri Baraka, 'The Changing Same' (1967) and 'John Coltrane: Where Does Art Come From?' (1978); for theoretical discussion of this Afro-American poetics at the time of publication of *At the Bottom of the River*, see James A. Snead, 'Repetition As A Figure of Black Culture' in Henry Louis Gates, *Black Literature and Literary Theory*, London: Pantheon Books, 1985.

15   Henry Louis Gates, 'The Blackness of Blackness' in *Black Literature and Literary Theory*, 285-321.

16   Anne Tyler, 'Mothers and Mysteries' in New Republic, 189 (Dec 31, 1983): 32-33; Edith Milton, 'Making a Virtue of Diversity' in *New York Times Book Review*, 89 (Jan 15, 1984): 22; Suzanne Freeman, 'Three Short Story Collections With a Difference' in *Ms*, 12 (Jan 1984): 15-16.

17   Helen Pyne Timothy, 'Adolescent Rebellion and Gender Relations in *At the Bottom of the River* and *Annie John*' in Selwyn R. Cudjoe, ed., *Caribbean Women Writers*, Calaloux, 1990.

18   Alison Donnell, 'When Daughters Defy: Jamaica Kincaid's Fiction' in *Women: A Cultural Review*, 4:1 (Spring 1993): 18-26.

19   Lizabeth Paravisini-Gebert, *Jamaica Kincaid*, p. 83.

20   See Isobel Hoving, *In Praise of New Travelers*, Stanford: Stanford UP, 2001, pp.186-203.

21   An earlier version of this section was published as Giovanna Covi, 'Jamaica Kincaid and the Resistance to Canons.'

22   John Bemrose, 'Growing Pains of Girlhood' in Macleans, 98 (May 20, 1985), p. 61; Bruce Van Wyngarden, 'First Novel' in *Saturday Review*, 11 (May/June 1985), p. 68; Patricia O'Connor, 'My Mother Wrote My Life' in *New York Times Book Review*, 90 (Apr. 7, 1985), p. 6.

23   Laura Niesen de Abruna, 'Jamaica Kincaid's Writing and the Maternal-Colonial Matrix' in Mary Condé and Thorunn Lonsdale, eds., *Caribbean Women Writers: Fiction in English*, New York: St. Martin's, 1999:172-183, p. 172.

24   Luce Irigaray, in *Ethique de la difference sexuelle*, Paris: Minuit, 1985; Julia Kristeva, 'Women's Time' in N.O. Keohane, M. Z. Rosaldo, and B.C. Gelpi, eds., *Feminist Theory: A Critique of Ideology*, Chicago: University of Chicago Press, 1982: 31-54.

25   Carole Boyce Davies, 'Writing Home: Gender and Heritage in the Works of Afro-Caribbean/American Women Writers' in *Out of the Kumbla*, 59-74, p. 62

26   Roland Barthes, 'The Death of the Author' in Stephen Heath, ed., *Image, Music, Text*, London: Fontana, 1977, p. 147.

27   Evelyn O'Callaghan, *Woman Version: Theoretical Approaches to West Indian Fiction by Women*, London: MacMillan, 1993, p. 59.

28   Published in an earlier version as 'The Islands in New York: Jamaica Kincaid's *Lucy*' in Erhard Reckwitz, Lucia Vennarini, Cornelia Wegener, eds., *Traditionalism vs. Modernism*, Essen: Die Blaue Eule, 1994: 257-270, and as 'Jamaica Kincaid's Prismatic Self and the Decolonaization of Language and Thought' in Joan Anim-Addo, ed., *Framing the World: Gender and Genre in Caribbean Women Writing*, London: Whiting and Birch, 1996: 37-68.

29   Kenneth Ramchad, 'West Indian Literary History: Literariness, Orality and Periodization' in *Callaloo*, 11:1 (Winter 1988): 95-110, p. 110.

30   Jamaica Kincaid with Leslie Garis, 'Through West Indian Eyes,' Interview in *New York Times Magazine*, Oct. 7, 1990: 42-44, 70, 78, 80, 91, p. 78.

31   Leslie Garis, 'Through West Indian Eyes,' p. 78.

32   Jamaica Kincaid with Sidonie Smith, *A Poetics of Women's Autobiography*, pp. 174-5. In Kincaid's case, the deconstruction of woman and author involves also the notions of race and nation, as *The Autobiography of My Mother* dramatically demonstrates.

33   Sidonie Smith, *A Poetics of Women's Autobiography*, p. 57.

34   Jamaica Kincaid with Leslie Garis, 'Through West Indian Eyes,' Interview, pp. 80, 91.

35   Moira Ferguson, *Jamaica Kincaid: Where the Land Meets the Body*, University of Virginia Press, 1994, p. 131. Ferguson's emphasis is on the relation of *Lucy* to *Annie John* and on its significance with regards to the fact that the narrator and protagonist begins to write. Diane Simmons, *Jamaica Kincaid*, New York: Twayne, 1994, places her interpretative emphasis on Lucy's strength to bear her solitude in the foreign country where she can become her own person.

36   See Linda Alcoff, 'Cultural Feminism vs. Poststructuralism: The Identity Crisis in Feminist Theory' in *Signs* 13:3 (1988): 405-36; Teresa de Lauretis, *Feminist Studies/ Critical Studies*, Bloomington: Indiana University Press, 1986; Gayatri C. Spivak, in Sarah Harasym, ed., *The Post-Colonial Critic: Interviews, Strategies, Dialogues*, New York: Routledge, 1990; Trinh T. Minh-ha, *Woman, Native, Other: Writing Postcoloniality and Feminism*, Bloomington: Indiana University Press, 1989.

37   Jane Gallop, 'Annie Leclerc Writing a Letter, with Vermeer' in Nancy K. Miller, ed., *The Poetics of Gender*, New York: Columbia UP, 1986: 137-156, p. 154.

38   Jamaica Kincaid with Louise Kennedy, 'A Writer Retraces Her Steps' Interview in *Boston Globe*, Nov. 7, 1990: 85, 89, p. 89.

39   See John McGowan, *Postmodernism and Its Critics*, Ithaca: Cornell University Press, 1991, for this definition of art in the modern age.

40   Jamaica Kincaid with Louise Kennedy, 'A Writer Retraces Her Steps,' p. 89.

41   Helen Tiffin, 'Cold Hearts and (Foreign) Tongues' in *Callaloo*, 16:3 (1993): 909-921, p. 921.

42   See Joseph Kronick, 'Hermeneutics and Literary Biography' in *boundary2*, 12:3/13:1 (Spring/Fall 1984): 99-120, for a discussion of auto/biography as expression of a humanistic notion of the individual, and Julia Kristeva, 'Woman Can Never Be Defined' in Elaine Marks and Isabelle de Courtivron, eds. *New French Feminisms*, New York: 137-144.

43   John McGowan, *Postmodernism and Its Critics*, pp. 88, 19 and 15, respectively.

44   Audre Lorde, 'Poetry is Not a Luxury' in *Sister Outsider*, Trumansburg, New York: Crossing, 1984, p. 37.

45   See Teresa de Lauretis, *Technologies of Gender: Essays on Theory, Film and Fiction*, Bloomington: Indiana University Press, 1987, p. 25.

46   I agree with Antonia MacDonald-Smythe, *Making Homes in the West Indies*, that 'Kincaid accepts her mother's constant voice as a given and uses it to propel herself into further artistic consciousness' (p. 99). Other readings of Kincaid's stories of childhood and adolescence emphasise the empowering force of the mother for Annie/Lucy's development as an assertive, independent anti-colonial speaking subject; see, for example: Susheila Nasta, 'Motherlands, Mother Cultures, Mother Tongues' in C.C. Barfoot and Theo D'haen, ed. *Shades of Empire*, Amsterdam: Rodopi, 1993, pp. 211-220; James Nagel, 'Desperate Hopes, Desperate Lives' in Melvin J. Friedman and Ben Siegel, *Traditions, Voices and Dreams*, Newark: University of Delaware Press, 1995, pp. 237-253; Craig Topping, 'Children and History in the Caribbean Novel' in *Kunapipi* XI:2 (1989), pp.51-59. More forcefully, Helen Scott, 'Dem Tief, Dem a Dam Tief' in *Callaloo* 25, 3(2002): 977-989, emphazies 'the absolute certainty about the determinant structures of inequality' in Kincaid's narrations and insists that her perspective is framed by the 'causal discourse of history rather than the postmodern 'weak thought' (p.988).

47   Gayatri C. Spivak, *A Critique of Postcolonial Reason*, p. x.

48   For a discussion of these implications, see Bruce Robbins, 'Soul Making: Gayatri Spivak on Upward Mobility' in *Cultural Studies*, 17:1 (2003):16-26.

49   Audre Lorde, 'Poetry is Not a Luxury,' p.35.

Chapter Three

Living and Dying: the Other Speaking as Subject

The Autobiography of My Mother-
My Brother-Mr. Potter

Jamaica Kincaid constantly writes and re-writes about her own life in Antigua, at the centre of which are the powerful feelings that characterize her relationship with her mother, as exemplified in *At the Bottom of the River*, *Annie John* and *Lucy*. The events of her life can be seen as marked by the contradictory sensations related to three fundamental separations from her mother and associated with her intellectual education. In addition, her elaboration of personal experience is always imbued with words, memories, and events related to her mother.

At nine, Kincaid left Antigua for Dominica to live with her Carib grandmother for a while because she was no longer the only child of a mother who had always loved to read to her and had taught her to read and write starting at age three. Dominica is the country her own mother, in turn, left at sixteen to go live in Antigua. At thirteen, with the birth of her third half-brother and the illness of her step-father, she was denied the education she had been taught to praise and expect during her infancy and, at sixteen, she was sent to the US as an au pair to help support her family. Here, she soon realized that her life had been interrupted for someone else's mistakes; she stopped sending money home and began supporting herself through school, instead: at twenty-four, she became a writer and changed her name from Elaine Cynthia Potter Richardson to Jamaica Kincaid; she would not return home nor speak to her mother for nearly twenty years. When she finally returned to Antigua in 1985, at thirty-six, she was informally expelled by the authorities, an experience recorded in *A Small Place*. Her following visits home — recalled in *My Brother* — were due to her brother's illness, and eventual death from AIDS. Moreover, as *Mr. Potter* sharply emphasizes, her entire life is a story which she can tell as a reaction to, or repetition of her own mother's words.[1]

Kincaid's continuous rewriting of her own life in terms of a conflictual confrontation with her mother and country of birth certainly goes beyond the personal claiming of her rights to independence and emancipation: her individual struggle for liberation from economic and cultural restrictions vindicates not only a history of gender discrimination, racial oppression, and colonial subjugation, but also persistently dismantles the ideological foundations that have allowed for the imposition of sexual, racial, and imperial hierarchies in modern times. Her discourse poignantly contributes to the creation of a new culture which resists historical as well as present forms of domination, through a continuous process of 're-memorying,' which allows for former oppression to shape present liberation and resistance and to conceive subjectivities that, however temporary and changeable, are fully conscious of the forces of power that threaten to reduce them to subaltern positions, precisely because they are grounded on those facts of history — personal and collective — which cannot and should not be erased.

The epistemic perspective Kincaid has been developing in the course of her works seeks in always richer and more complex ways, to offer new parameters for articulating knowledge in our times: Kincaid aptly describes this narrative movement in her works as 'musical.'[2] In her most recent narrations, what is sharpened, clarified, intensified, and thus rendered more complexly is her radical revision of the philosophical foundations of the discourse of Modernity, which has supported the rise of Western colonialism and still influences large parts of contemporary 'post-colonial' cultures. I would argue that such revisionary force and devastating critique are imbued with a Caribbean perspective, and not because of seductively reductionist descriptions of the Caribbean as unchartable territory, but rather because of the socio-historical specificity of the region and its political impact on the past and present world order.[3] At the same time, I would argue against casting the Caribbean as an icon for a metaphysical status of in-betweenness, a sort of crossroad where all the dichotomies find their point of encounter and pre-given solution.[4] On the contrary, the Caribbean for Kincaid represents a referent which greatly contributes to grounding in a local socio-historical context her inventive cultural creations by providing a truthfully realistic referent for her theoretical meditations which, otherwise, transcend national boundaries and cross over cultural specificities to articulate the larger frame for an epistemic and ontological new understanding of present culture. M. Nourbese Philip asks, 'How does one make something, anything — a land, a language, a history, a place in time — truly one's own' and suggests that 'A poet must, often uneasily, often tentatively, find her own unique answer to the question of place, be it through language, through connectedness with a particular geographical locale, or through an understanding and acceptance of a particular historical experience.'[5] Kincaid poses her own unique answer by combining these perspectives together. She provides the words to express the present need for an epistemological break when she refuses the standard opposition between fiction and reality and insists that her historical perspective is 'truthful' rather than 'factual.'[6] The truth she is telling is variously characterized by anger, as in *The Autobiography of My Mother*, despair, as in *My Brother*, or indifference, as in *Mr. Potter*, but it is invariably fostered by her commitment to making sense of her own being in the world, inside and outside a pre-defined modernity.

Her dedication to sense-making is fuelled by her incessant effort to relentlessly challenge further and further the possibility of saying the yet-unsaid. This represents Kincaid's participation in what Angela Carter calls the 'decolonialization of language and thought' — an endless commitment, a 'slow process.' Carter indicates that it 'has nothing to do with being a legislator of humankind'; rather, it works towards bringing what Edward Said has defined as 'affiliations' within a particular historical context through risking language and questioning logic.[7] These two concepts, *decolonialization* and *affiliations*, help me clarify the significance of the role played by language/rhetoric in the production of social agency and of subjectivity; they clarify and intensify the meaning of the ethical-political concepts of *accountability*, *responsibility* and *sustainability*, which have been increasingly developed to counter dominating global forces of power.[8] Kincaid's questioning of logic and epistemology makes this ethical commitment even clearer and more material. I would argue that, through the rhythms of writing whose repetitive patterns are oral and whose syntax is seemingly as simple as a child's, she increasingly allows us to see how to cope with the complexities of life today. Most importantly, she does so without indulging in the delusion of conquering death, a need which Wilson Harris has shown to be connected to a history of conquests, inquisitions, racism, and rape. Indeed, Kincaid writes in what

Harris calls 'the epic voice of arrival,' which is poetic and historical rather than metaphysical, the voice of relational identity which may not tell us always what we like to hear but which does not need to produce death in order to remove it away from life.[9] Instead, this voice is focused on birth, and on the maternal who lives through narrating herself rather than through conquering death. Unlike the classical myth of Orpheus, her poetic voice does not need a dead woman to sing its love to: its relational need can be satisfied by singing its everyday happiness to its interlocutor, Eurydice, who makes that love and the uniqueness of the lovers possible.[10] Kincaid's philosophy merging into poetry, a necessity and 'not a luxury,' thus subverts and expands our epistemological and ontological boundaries and grounds existence in birth, rather than in an impossible transcendental struggle against death. By doing so, it fully accepts being grounded in the narrative act and inexorably becoming dialogically relational. In its diversity and nevertheless by virtue of its inescapable social implications, Kincaid's lyrical voice runs parallel with research and expression more explicitly integrated with a process of liberation that moves beyond national liberation to foresee a global context that is increasingly decentred and in which it is possible to theorize and practice an alterity/subjectivity without risking appropriation and exclusion. Her theorizing is strictly linked to her risk-taking empirical work as a writer and thus reaches the strategic effect Spivak invokes when she disclaims 'theories of essences.'[11]

The *Autobiography of My Mother*, *My Brother* and *Mr Potter* articulate a perspective that embraces complexity from multiple positions, marking an engagement with the comprehensive view expressed in *My Garden(Book):*. While the earlier autobiographical stories present the confrontation of Kincaid's Subject with the otherness of the outside world, in these (auto)biographical stories Kincaid accepts the challenge to listen to and give voice to the Others of her own Subject, thus engaging the difficult task of turning otherness itself into subjectivity. In other words, she tests the limits structurally imposed upon the utterance of the subaltern. In this sense, these (auto)biographical narratives of her relatives forcefully subvert the colonial writing of the discovery and possession of the 'other'/'new' world: their stance not only goes beyond a simple reversal of the imperial point of view; it also voices the implications of a rewriting of history that liberates the subject from colonial and patriarchal as well as from cultural domination. It does so by fostering identities that never rest on the newly-found place and never turn it into a monumental, promised land; rather, they keep passing from place to place, as well as through time and space, and they also mimetically pass for another person; in the process, they engage in acts of 're-memorying,' thus turning their past oppression into knowledge and empowerment to fight present discrimination.[12] By necessity rather than for promoting a certain identity politics, these subjectivities thus cast a gaze on their own past, into their own origin instead of aiming at an idealized goal in the future: they accept not only the challenge of looking into the mystery of 'who' they are rather than resting on a given definition of 'what' they should be, but also the formidable challenge of giving voice to those who in the course of history have either tried to annihilate them or have been silenced by socio-historical conditions of oppression. Indeed the narratives about Kincaid's family attempt the seemingly impossible and yet necessary task of making the subalterns speak through her own writing without either speaking for them or reducing them to native informants.

The Autobiography of My Mother (1996)[13]

Xuela in *The Autobiography of My Mother* accepts the challenge of making the voiceless heard when she states: 'Who you are is a mystery no one can answer, not even you. And why not, why not!' (*A* 202). Through this self-consciousness, the subject may achieve its liberation from a subaltern position. This is why *The Autobiography* takes us on a more difficult and unfamiliar path than, for example, *Lucy*. While Lucy accepts/transforms/re-memories her own name, the narrator in *The Autobiography* tackles the question of coming to terms with history from a theoretical point of view while asking herself not only 'who am I in relation to others,' but also 'who is my own alterity?' It does so by explicitly redefining history as discourse: at the end of what she aptly calls her 'sermonette' (*A* 132-8), the narrator offers us more than a picture with commentary of a specific socio-cultural reality; in fact, she gives us also the theory that makes that picture so devastating when she says: 'for me history was not a large stage filled with commemorations ... with the sounds of victory. For me history was not only the past: it was the past and it was also the present' (*A* 138-9).

Conceiving history as discourse has broad implications on this text's portrayal of the world and of subjectivity in general. *The Autobiography* provides an exemplary model of Gayatri Spivak's concept of 'cultural translation', a concept I extend to include a definition of feminist theory, which is always also practice. As translated subjectivity, a self is conceived as a passing entity, circulating among different contexts and never frozen into the transcendental icon of a fixed identity. Like history, subjectivity is discursive. As such, it retains the rhetoricity of language and it works in the silent spaces between and around words. 'The jagged relation between rhetoric and logic,' Spivak points out, 'as condition and effect of knowing, allows the world to be made of an agent who acts in it in an ethical, a political, a day-to-day way.' This is why translated thinking 'forces us to say things for which no language previously existed.'[14] Kincaid can be said to write as a cultural translator — not a native informant — when she declares: 'For me writing is a revelation. If I knew what it would be then it would be of no interest for me to do it ... I know how it works, but I haven't quite said it yet. The minute that I'm conscious of it then it's of no interest.'[15]

In Kincaid's works, and specifically in *The Autobiography* and *My Brother*, this radically translated thinking takes apart the structuring features of Modernity — namely, the colonization and genderization of culture — by uprooting its notions of history and death. It is from this philosophical perspective that I disagree with most of the reviewers of *The Autobiography* and *My Brother*, even the sympathetic ones, who constantly foreground a 'dark' tone of 'desolation,' 'despair,' or even 'wrath,' 'scorn,' 'inhuman narcissism' and 'contempt' in its pages. I find that Kincaid's writing compellingly demands not to be taken at face value.[16]

Reading, for example, *The Autobiography* as a discursive articulation of a feminist subjectivity in a specific cultural and socio-historical context, rather than as the account of a personal life, allows me to foreground not only its historical value — Xuela as a metaphorical representation of the experience of the African diaspora and of the genocide of the Carib Indians[17] — but also its epistemological impact, its positive propositional force. Rather than the despair of the narrator's life, in Xuela I am driven to read the rejection of an Americanized cultural viewpoint that sentimentally forces happy endings upon the common hardships of life. Kincaid invites this reading when she states that her existential view is 'fierce' rather than 'desolate,' because it accounts for the fact that life is always hard and complicated.[18] She reiterates this invitation also when she criticizes 'the pursuit of happiness' in *The American Declaration of*

Independence by calling it a meaningless, 'bad little sentence,' because, she observes, happiness cannot be willingly pursued.[19]

Explicitly and from the beginning, *The Autobiography* demands that we rid ourselves of the structuring dichotomy governing the prose narratives of Modernity — the opposition between fact and fiction. One of the initial paragraphs in the book, in which the narrator tells us 'I was not afraid, because my mother had already died,' ends with the parenthetical observation: 'it is not really true that I was not afraid then.' The next paragraph begins with the following meta-narrative comment:

> If I speak now of those first days with clarity and insight, it is not an invention ... at the time, each thing as it took place stood out in my mind with a sharpness that I now take for granted; it did not then have a meaning, it did not have a context, I did not yet know the history of events... (*A* 15)

Clearly, the narration is governed by 'truth' and 'invention' — it is thus a discursive elaboration of personal experience into political, theoretical knowledge, which questions the separation between fact and fiction imposed upon literature by Modern culture.[20] It is a process of 're-memory' aimed at attributing political significance to personal experience, as the long passage introducing the Speaking-I and its indissoluble relation with her mother makes clear:

> My days were spent in a schoolhouse. This education I was receiving had never offered me the satisfaction I was told it would; it only filled me with questions that were not answered, it only filled me with anger. I could not like what it lead to: a humiliation so permanent that it would replace your own skin. And your own name, whatever it might be, eventually was not the gateway to who you really were, and you could not ever say to yourself, 'My name is Xuela Claudette Desvarieux.' This was my mother's name, but I cannot say it was her real name, for in a life like hers, as in mine, what is a real name? My own name is her name, Xuela Claudette, and in the place of the Desvarieux is Richardson, which is my father's name; but who are those people, Claudette, Desvarieux, and Richardson? To look into it, to look at it, could only fill you with despair; the humiliation could only make you intoxicated with self-hatred. For the name of any one person is at once her history recapitulated and abbreviated, and on declaring it, that person holds

herself high or low, and the person hearing it holds the declarer high or low.

My mother was placed outside the gates of a convent when she was perhaps a day old by a woman believed to be her own mother; she was wrapped in pieces of clean old cloth, and the name Xuela was written on these pieces of cloth; it was written in an ink whose color was indigo, a dye rendered from a plant. She was not discovered because she had been crying; even as a newborn she did not draw attention to herself. She was found by a woman, a nun who was on her way to wreak more havoc in the lives of the remnants of a vanishing people; her name was Claudette Desvarieaux. She named my mother after herself, she called my mother after herself; how the name Xuela survived I do not know, but my father gave it to me when she died, just after I was born. (A 78-80)

The cover page tells us that Xuela's story is a mixture of truth and invention, a description which inscribes its own understanding — 'the autobiography' is called 'a novel'; it is 'of my mother'; and it is 'by Jamaica Kincaid,' as if to expose the complications inherent in representational language. To me, nobody puts it in better words than Rikki Ducornet, when she describes this kind of discourse in the following terms:

Like the moon, the novel is a symbol and a necessary reality. Ideally, it serves neither gods nor masters. Philosopher's stone, it sublimates, precipitates and quickens. House of Keys, it opens all our darkest doors. May the Pol Pot Persons of all genders and denominations take heed: to create a fictional world with rigor and passion, to imagine a character of any sex, place, time, or color and make it palpitate and quiver, to catapult it into the deepest forests of our most luminous reveries, is to commit an act of empathy. To write a novel of the imagination is a gesture of tenderness; to enter into a book is a fearless act and generous.[21]

Fearless and generous, rather than angry and desolate are the most apt qualifications for Kincaid's oeuvre. Again, Ducornet reiterates it most effectively:

I insist: it is not only our right, but our responsibility to follow our imaginations' enchanted paths wherever they would lead us; to heed those voices that inhabit our most secret (and sacred) spaces. When in 1973 thousands were taken to Santiago Stadium ... Gabriel Garcia

Marquez, in an act of defiance and revulsion, ceased to write. After five years, he came to the conclusion that *only by writing could I oppose Pinochet. Without realizing it, I had sumitted myself to his censorship* (Nouvelle Observateur).[22]

Kincaid's *The Autobiography* is a rejection of censorship. The cover shows two photos: of a woman on the front and of the author on the back cover. Jamaica Kincaid's black and white photo is copyrighted by Marianne Cook in 1992, who authored *Generations of Women: In Their Own Words*, a collection of photos in black and white of grandmothers, mothers and daughters and their own self-descriptions, with an introduction by Kincaid. In Cook's volume, next to the picture of Kincaid with her mother and daughter, we read that grandmother Annie Drew from Dominica was raised by her father, which made her 'rough'; about her own daughter she says: 'Even if sometimes she may say one or two things that are fiction, I'm never vexed. As a writer, what she will write is just fiction.' Conversely, mother Jamaica Kincaid, after acknowledging 'powerful feelings of despair, dislike and even sometimes revulsion for [her own] mother' but also the impossibility of 'constructing a world without her,' observes: 'what's interesting about her story is that she's made a romance of her life.' Finally, Kincaid's daughter Annie Shawn, named after her grandmother, points out that 'sometimes [her own] mother acts like [her] grandmother.'[23] The photo shows this connection through young Annie: it intensifies the intellectual effort to understand the relational meaning of these three different lives and the subjectivities they have shaped. It is a mixture of 'truth' and 'invention,' storytelling which is making history, biographies woven into autobiographies.

The sepia picture on the front cover is repeated in the text to mark the otherwise untitled, unnumbered chapters: it gradually builds up from what looks like ripped copies into a final full portrait. This photo is not given copyright acknowledgment. We assume it is the mother of the title until the narrator tells us her mother died before she knew her, and the narrator never even saw a picture of her face. Xuela's mother — herself named Xuela — is a cloth with her name written on (A 79), heels sticking out of a white gown (A 18), the hem of a long dress (A 31) — she is all this in her daughter's dreams, and nothing else. She remains only a dress even when the daughter tries to imagine her:

a dress made of nankeen, a loose-fitting dress, a shroud; it covered her arms, her knees, it fell all the way down to her ankles. She wore a matching piece of cloth on her head that covered all her beautiful hair completely ... she carried a bundle on the top of her head ... (A 200)

The 'bundle' on her head takes us back to the initial scene where the speaking Xuela is a 'bundle,' indistinguishable from the 'bundle' of her father's 'soiled clothes' given to Eunice, her foster mother, to wash (A 4). The 'dress made of nankeen,' instead, reminds us of the cloth into which Eunice folds the washed and ironed clothes of Xuela's father (A 6). The same material marks the steps of Xuela's growth: the 'drawers' of a dead man she wears during the androgynous phase in her life (A 98), and the nightgown her father gave her which she wears during her first sexual encounter with Philip (A 151). This fabric figuratively seals the relation between the two women, even though Xuela never gets to know her homonymous mother and wonders: 'And this woman whose face I have never seen, not even in a dream — what did she think?' (A 201). Nevertheless, in the end she acknowledges:

This account of my life has been an account of my mother's life as much as it has been an account of mine, and even so, again it is an account of the life of the children I did not have, as it is their account of me. In me is the voice I never heard, the face I never saw, the being I came from. In me are the voices that should have come out of me, the faces I never allowed to form, the eyes I never allowed to see me. This account is an account of the person who was never allowed to be and an account of the person I did not allow myself to become. (A 227-8)

This encourages me to interpret the cover photo as that of the narrator in her mother's clothes and this novel as a self-reflexive discourse aimed at foregrounding the political function of rhetoric (clothes in this case) in the social constitution of subjectivity. Sidonie Smith theorizes that women's autobiographies are not written against one's own mother-rather, they parallel the life of one's mother; Luce Irigaray and differently Judith Butler argue that feminist personal writing is grounded in narration and birth and for this reason it runs counter to the patriarchal tradition which, starting from Oedipus, has conceived subjectivity as written against its own mother and pursuing the defeat of death through immortality; Lorna Goodison states the need for a woman to become 'her own mother,' in order to become herself, birth herself, re-invent herself.[24] Xuela's is the autobiography of a woman who is 'becoming her own mother' — her metamorphosis is meant to celebrate the creativity and continuity of birth as the creative potential to re-define herself.[25] Jamaica Kincaid repeatedly insists that writing is drawn from her need to investigate her own life whose origin, she fully acknowledges, is in her own mother.[26]

That Xuela investigates her own life to elaborate it into writing is underlined by the widespread use of clothes as a figure for socio-psychological descriptions. The father is, rather than wears, a jailer's uniform (A 39, 50, 90); the frustrated great aspiration in his life is reduced to owning an English suit, which is all he has to offer to his own son as a model of his personality (A 54). The dramatic incidents in the life of Xuela — a 'bundle' at the beginning — are all marked by her possession and refusal of certain dresses. Most significant is the episode in which Xuela and Madame La Batte communicate perfectly without words and by putting Lise's clothes on and taking them off instead (A 69). It is by consistently refusing to wear these clothes that Xuela understands her imposed function in the La Batte's household and rebels against it; her opposition to the La Battes' domination is represented by the independence of her erotic will when unclothed (A 69) and by renouncing her child when wearing a deadman's clothes (A 98). Xuela's sexuality is expressed in sadomasochistic terms, which could be read as aiming at subverting the representation of colonial domination.[27]

Xuela exposes the misery and the pretense of the 'simple' (A 67), 'reduced' (A 223) truths of the colonial order by exposing the falseness of the clothes of the people — teachers, father, stepmother, sister, and husband — who represent such order. For instance, Philip, her husband, although he is the only person who says he loves her, is reduced to 'a book,' 'a blue shirt' (A 149), and a pair of beige linen trousers (A 151) when he accepts her seduction. His clothes, like his passion for the classifications in natural science, always leave out something and transform the truth, which 'is always so full of uncertainty' (A 223), into a 'pretty picture' — like that of the congregation in front of the church, which must leave Lazarus out (A 142). Xuela does not buy into this 'Enlightened' epistemological frame which has supported the imposition of racial, sexual, and national discrimination throughout the world. Xuela fully understands the subjugation that occurs when female beings are divided into 'women' and 'ladies' (*A* 159), and when humanity is separated into 'men' and 'people' (*A* 226). For this reason, she marries but neither in order to become a wife (a man's lady) nor a mother (how can she, having been denied one herself?); she marries, on the contrary, only after she has recognized that romance (the kingdom of love) is 'the refuge of the defeated' and after she has observed: 'I believe my life was without love' (*A* 216). And yet she does marry and works out a lasting relationship with Philip. Her whole existence vindicates the subordinate role to which the Other is confined by the supremacy of Reason and Individualism by dismantling such order and claiming 'fiercely' a different set of values.[28] Diane Simmons, who calls *The Autobiography* a 'brutal book,' interprets the relationship between Xuela and Philip to mean that they are locked in a history that forbids them to be happy.[29] Isabel Hoving, declaring that Kincaid's anger 'seems to reach its peak' in this book, also reads in Xuela's story a 'refusal of history.'[30] Laura Niesen de Abruna laments that it lacks the warmth that characterizes Lucy and considers it a fiction aimed at expressing resentment of colonialism and at claiming maternal death.[31] On the contrary and in agreement with Alison Donnel, I would argue that Xuela is capable of expressing empowerment both of the self and of the other: 'It is in Xuela's story that her mother's will be told, and in Kincaid's text that her own mother's narrative will find expression' and becomes 'a form of decolonisation and dehegemonisation.'[32]

Xuela's experience brings her to realize that 'love' is indistinguishable from its opposite (*A* 22); she fights her oppression by learning to love what she is told to hate (*A* 32). Education will soon bring her the awareness that love cannot inhabit a history of humiliation, enslavement, and mistrust (*A* 48). Thus she will learn to love 'in defiance,' which is a love that 'will do but only do' (*A* 56) and tastes 'rancid' (*A* 57). It recalls the taste of the 'sour' (*A* 5) milk of her foster mother Eunice, which was nevertheless better than the 'bitter' tea, 'moldy' food (*A* 29) and 'poisonous' necklace (*A* 33) given to her by her stepmother, a fairy tale-like wicked creature recalling the gothic tone of 'Ovando'. Even her love 'beyond words' (*A* 176) for a man whose mouth looked 'like an island' (*A* 164), Roland, must come to an end, because it is deceitful and 'dangerous' (*A* 178); the dream for this impossible love story comes alive precisely 'in the moments when' the 'pleasure' of making love with her husband 'waned': 'My mind turned to another source of pleasure. He was a man that was Philip's opposite. His name was Roland' (*A* 163).

Xuela chooses the Englishman Philip as her husband and does not regret her choice; neither does she present it as a desperate choice, and not even the sign of her defeat: in a way comparable to the realization reached by Sethe in Morrison's *Beloved*, under circumstances that are possibly even more extreme, Xuela does not believe herself to be 'nothing' (*A* 226) because of her capacity to negotiate a space for her own subjectivity in the difficult context in which she succeeds in exercising agency. Rather, she shows us the significance of a troubled existence lived by refusing to rely on myths, ideologies, and beliefs. Her subjectivity is never an identity conceived as a being identical to oneself — rather, it is an indentity understood as identification; it is not an identical identity even when she sternly states, 'I was myself' (*A* 167). This becomes clear when we compare the child Xuela, who shatters Eunice's platter thus rejecting that the English countryside painted on it represents Heaven (*A* 8-9), with the adult Xuela, who self-consciously calls 'an identity' the choice to 'belong to a race' and a 'crime' the willingness to 'accept a nation' (*A* 226). While for her choice she pays the price of not bearing children, it is clear that her self certainly refuses to be reduced to desolation. K. T. Mcguire laments that there is 'no resurrection' in *The Autobiography*, and Tai Moses complains that Xuela 'lacks recognizable human traits' and the book offers 'no redemption' to her and 'no catharsis' to her readers.[33] On the contrary, I would rather applaud the absence of resurrection, redemption, and catharsis as evidence that Kincaid's discourse moves within other parameters than those offered by this metaphysical tradition.

The 'bundle' on her head takes us back to the initial scene where the speaking Xuela is a 'bundle' (*A* 4), capable in the end of acknowledging that, 'This account of my life has been an account of my mother's life as much as it has been an account of mine' (*A* 227). This remark allows me to interpret the cover photo as that of the narrator in her mother's clothes, an intimate cultural translation of her own historical mother and the rejection of a myth of origin, or the belief in a mother-goddess.[34] Indeed, this novel is throughout a self-reflexive discourse aimed at foregrounding the political function of rhetoric (photographs and clothes capture charactes just like translated words attempt to render the human experience) in the social constitution of subjectivity.[35] Xuela is a subject who needs neither to kill her mother nor to annihilate herself in order to exist as an identity: when, in Lorna Goodison's poem 'I Am Becoming My Mother,' we read 'my mother is now me,' we understand the celebration of the creativity and continuity of birth as the generative potential to re-define oneself; likewise, when we read about the mother in Xuela's narrative, we see the narrator's creative and self-generative potential. Xuela does not linger in her despair; rather, she elaborates her tragedy to grow aware of the difficulties that mark the path going beyond it.

This is why the cover photo becomes the appropriate referent for a self-referential meditation: this subjectivity states her own identity by retaining a sense of another, a consciousness underlined by the author's photograph meant to indicate the theoretical and thus political value of Xuela's personal account. It is thus not surprising that this novel, whose subject matter is so explicitly personal, is dedicated to Derek Walcott rather than, say, to Kincaid's own Dominican mother and Carib Indian grandmother. The dedication elevates autobiography out of the personal boundaries and into the realm of cultural production, so that the insistence on the Dominican setting and the detailed descriptions of nature on the island carry also an echo of Jean Rhys's *Wide Sargasso Sea*. More compellingly than being a tribute to the Caribbean cultural and literary heritage to which Kincaid's philosophical and international discourse wants to and does belong — observe the intensity with which the loss of one's mother reverberates with the unspeakable suffering of slavery and massacre — these references dismantle the figuration of the Caribbean as the Other of Europe or the Other America, and open it up to the fluid space in which the sea flows to connect the islands among themselves and to the rest of the world.[36] As Rhonda Cobham pointedly underlines, through a detailed and well-informed critical analysis of the relationship between African culture and Creole gnosis, Xuela is willing to risk 'social annihilation in order to claim for herself the right to exist in the landscape that has produced her and in which she has learned to survive and understand the human condition ... [this world] has real limits and no originary innocence ... but it need not be a world of silence and fear.'[37] *The Autobiography*, Cobham concludes, forces postcolonial criticism beyond the trivial simplification that opposes alien dominant culture to enabling folk culture.

Knowledge as cultural elaboration of experience, an experience of suffering and deprivation, comes in the absence of resurrection, redemption, and catharsis. I would applaud this absence as evidence that Kincaid's discourse explores the possibilities offered to a thinking which is poetic and historical at the same time and risks not telling us

JAMAICA KINCAID'S PRISMATIC SUBJECTS: MAKING SENSE OF BEING IN THE WORLD

always what we would like to hear because, like Wilson Harris's 'epic voice of arrival,' it accepts the challenge to live without the need to conquer death.[38] When memory engages the slow process of re-memorying and decolonializing, when it challenges language and identity in order to explore new epistemic possibilities, the hope for a world no longer ruled by the impulse to conquer and control death starts taking shape.

My Brother (1998)

On January 19, 1996, Kincaid's youngest half-brother, Devon, died of AIDS; he was only thirty-three. At the time she was finishing *The Autobiography*, which focuses so repeatedly on the meaning of death. In *My Brother*, she explores even more sharply the boundaries of subjectivity in its confrontation with death, describing Devon's illness and death in Antigua. But the book is not so much about her brother as about the effort engaged by the speaking subject to distill her personal experience in order to make sense of death. This text addresses the infinitely simple, yet overwhelmingly complex question: 'if it is so certain, death, why is it such a surprise?' (*MB* 193). Kincaid's articulation of this question has provocative and challenging cultural implications, which subvert traditional figurations of life's struggle against death. *My Brother* engages some of the issues which Adriana Cavarero clearly articulates in what she labels 'philosophy of narration,' uprooting the epistemological frame that makes such figuration possible.[39] Sarah Brophy rightly observes how the self-theorizing performed in this 'melancholic text' provides 'a rethinking of the politics of grief that is relevant and bracing for theoretical discussions of postcolonial and racial mourning, as well as for coming to grips with the cultural impact of the AIDS pandemic as it continues to follow the fault lines of globalization.'[40] In her sharp discussion of the meaning of melancholy in the context of postcolonial studies, Brophy warns against simply associating melancholy with compensatory guilt and nostalgia and suggests instead to consider the relationship between the decentred quality of melancholic subjectivity and memory; thus melancholy is interpreted as a sign of Kincaid's politicized discourse and Devon is seen as the embodiment of her political unconscious, representing both identification and exclusion.[41] I fully share this perspective that underlines Kincaid's willingness to face complexity even when it is so painful, as I endorse the observation that the effort to analyze her feelings about her brother imply 'that there may not be a life (her own or Devon's) to reconstruct as would ordinarily be conceived of in the conventions of Western biography or autobiography.'[42]

In *My Brother*, the speaking voice's elaboration of experience into knowledge produces a discourse which is simultaneously diegetic and mimetic; it gives us a history which is also poetry, and thus is epic; consequently, it articulates a subjectivity which, by existing only relationally, says at the same time the 'who' — unnamable and unchangeable — and the 'what' — definable and multiple — of its own being in the world. Storytelling itself is not essential to relational subjectivity; rather, it expresses the essential need for telling itself to others. It is instead autobiography which becomes an impossibility for this subjectivity: its identity being conceived as an ontological uniqueness which needs a relational context; its 'I' being constructed by its desire to hear a 'You' (an Other) tell its own uniqueness in the form of a story capable of weaving the namable, plural, and changeable 'what' with the ineffable, fixed, and singular 'who' of one's existence. The story which the Other tells to the One mixes conceptual definitions with undefinable passions, the spirit with the body, death with life; it is never purely fictional nor factual, never personal nor objective.

Indeed, contrary to universalistic notions and individualistic identity which pursue a metaphysical unity (attainable indeed only by death) and which struggle to produce a text in the vain attempt to overcome death, relational identity does not desire such an immortal totalitarian text. As it has been conceptualized in various but similar ways by feminist theorists, it rather seeks a text which is inessential. Like translation, it is temporary and it speaks only because first it has listened. In addition, it speaks with the fully-accepted consciousness that 'death is the only reality, for it is the only certainty, inevitable to all things,' as we are reminded by the final sentence of *The Autobiography* (A 228). Instead of inhabiting the philosophical world, Adriana Cavarero observes, relational identity dwells in the Arendtian political scene of mutual exchange and is well aware that if it is true that life produces infinite stories, it is as well true that there is no story capable of returning a single life: Cavarero wittingly remarks that pure textuality, like the Cartesian cogito, has never, as it were, given birth to any children. Instead, relational identity pursues through action in the world a theoretical knowledge which is plural and collective. Grounded on the uniqueness of each birth which is its unnamable specificity, relational identity does not feel the need to overcome death because it does not set for itself the impossible goal of attaining unity.[43]

Kincaid's subjectivities are always relational: they express themselves in the epic terms of a poetry which is also history, even when the form of their expression is a political essay, as in *A Small Place,* or a lyrical story, as in 'Girl.' They cannot therefore speak of one identity only, and Kincaid's writing about her life is performed by a narrator who tells back her story to the author, by a Speaking-I who understands herself differently in different contexts but always in relation to her own origin — the unnamable, unchangeable 'who' — which is her own mother. This is why a book on the death of the author's brother cannot be about the brother — just like the one on the mother is not about the mother — but must instead be about the re-telling by the narrator of the author's relational identity under the circumstances of her brother's death.

As in *The Autobiography,* the images that accompany and are an integral part of this text exemplify this point. The cover looks like a photo album: black capital letters on a white page announce 'MY BROTHER' on top and 'JAMAICA KINCAID' below a sepia-colored snapshot pasted obliquely on it with ripped black tape; it figures a person reading something cut off from the picture frame and sitting in front of a wood house in the tropics, under the scanty shade of some palm leaves.[44] The photo is copyrighted by Jamaica Kincaid and it is reproduced in fainted black-and-white on the back cover, where it provides the background for the following statement, a passage from the book:

> I became a writer out of desperation, so when I first heard my brother was dying I was familiar with the act of saving myself: I would write ... make an attempt at understanding his dying .... (Back cover and *MB* 197)

The indication 'out of desperation' is clear: this book is meant neither as a realistic, objective piece, the biography of an Other, nor as an intimate, introspective narrative, the quest for one's Self. Rather, it forces writing to tread the territory where language describes what is known and discovers the yet unknown and unsaid at the same time: it walks on the epic soil where poetry and history meet. The narrator states explicitly that what she is writing is 'a narrative form' (*MB* 188) and 'not a journal'

(*MB* 91): it does not have the immediacy of 'a daily account' because the subject matter needed distance, the work of 'memory' (*MB* 167), in order to be written. She thus 'sits and contemplates' her life in relation to others, and acknowledges how much 'the present shapes the past' and will also 'shape the future' (*MB* 167), thereby embracing the full implications of considering history as discourse articulated in *The Autobiography*.[45]

The actual act of writing and the customary detailed care Kincaid devotes to language as a material component of existence occupy a prominent position in this meditation. The quotation above, for example, is preceded by an equally explicit reference to language as materiality rather than as its reproduction, when the narrator states that 'it is life that produces metaphors' (*MB* 168). The meta-narrative interventions are at least as numerous as the direct references to Kincaid's activity as a writer during Devon's illness; she mentions explicitly: writing and then launching *The Autobiography* (*MB* 72, 151); quitting *The New Yorker* (*MB* 101) after many years; giving an interview (*MB* 100); she also remembers becoming a writer (*MB* 180), and she evaluates her own previous production by judging *A Small Place* full of 'futile ... denunciations' (*MB* 158).

Her contemplation narrates her brother's illness and then again his actual death by exact scientific descriptions and by the metaphorical use of various plants and trees whose life, death, reproduction, and whose dependence or not on somebody else's care explicitly express the personalities of narrator, brother, and mother, and their inter-relationships. But the linguistic aspect which most strictly connects this text to *The Autobiography* is the development of a metaphorical use of clothes throughout the narration. Her brother who didn't have the opportunity and couldn't find the strength to live his life as an agent is shown to wear just 'a plain chemise' (*MB* 5) as a newborn; he begs his sister for a pair of shorts she is wearing when he is ill (*MB* 76), and finally he is zipped up, 'like an expensive suit,' in a plastic bag as a dead body (*MB* 178). It is only in a photograph (which belongs to the family album and which significantly was not used as a cover for the book) that the brother in the beauty of his youth wears clothes made of 'precious fabric' (*MB* 93). And again in a recollection it is he as a young boy who 'liked to place patches of different colored cloth all over his clothes' (*MB* 171-2), so that the second brother, Dalma, came to call him 'Patches' (*MB* 175); and it is Devon, in turn, who gives the oldest brother the nickname 'Styles,' because he would always 'dress ... stylish' (*MB* 172). Fittingly, the narrator observes that she was 'never part of the tapestry, so to speak, of Patches, Styles and Muds' (*MB* 175), the last being the name Devon called his mother as a boy and then again as a dying man, while calling her Mrs. Drew, as did his other brother, for the rest of his adult life. Names and clothes mark the troubled relationships between the mother and all her children: relationships in which the infinite love the mother can give both her young and her sick and dependent children transforms itself into humiliation and not love when they are grown and independent.

This is why at Devon's funeral nobody wears a dress bought or made for the occasion, and the narrator wears a dress she had bought for an award-giving ceremony for her husband and then refused to wear (*MB* 168) — a rejected garment. By contrast, another family in the book, described burying a four-year-old boy, are dressed in clothes that match the loss of their 'pure love' (*MB* 145). Similar explicit attention is devoted to labelling the various registers of language — Creole, Standard English (*MB* 33), pretend English (*MB* 56), broken English (*MB* 33) — and to the terms used to talk about AIDS and homosexuality which for Kincaid's brother — a man incapable of facing his own life fully — remain 'that chupidness' (*MB* 8, 65) and 'auntie-men' (*MB* 147). But this oblique naming does not change the nature of things, as the narrator clearly observes apropos her brother's habit of smoking marijuana, which he calls 'the Weed ... as if that made it something harmless' (*MB* 112).

Death under these circumstances is thus written on, not written against. Reviewers have variously called this text 'bitter,' 'scathing,' 'soaked in the stale emotions of a scalded psyche,' an 'irritating navel-contemplation,' and lamented its lack of 'mercy' and 'empathy.'[46] I would argue, instead, that this act of dealing straightforwardly with death is not bleak in and of itself but rather a positive propositional subversive stance, which shows the way to rid ourselves of what Wilson Harris rightly indicates as being at the roots of a history of conquest, rape, and inquisitions: namely, the impulse to conquer death, which is so pervasive as to be equated to the resurrection of Christ.[47] Harris calls for a re-imagination in the form of a re-birth of epic-epic as arrival, as transfiguration versus photographic description. Reading Harris's epic voice of arrival, can provide the frame for understanding Kincaid's relational identity.[48]

The new epic voice, which is poetic and historical rather than metaphysical, is the voice of relational identity that may not always tell us what we like to hear — it indeed upsets readers trapped in a Hollywood-like ethics of good feelings and happy endings, and correct lines, who call for 'mercy,' 'forgiveness,' 'empathy,' even 'decorum,' or even consumeristically for something 'new,'[49] as if life could ever provide a new plot. Kincaid grasps that new stories are not necessarily made of new material, and she writes about subjectivity in its fluid movement in the world. Unlike the classical myth of Orpheus, her poetic voice does not need a dead woman to sing its love: its relational need would be satisfied by singing its everyday happiness to the interlocutor, Eurydice, who makes that love and the uniqueness of the lovers possible. Eurydice neither needs to be confined to the Underworld nor rescued to this one as nothing more than a pawn of Death — a liberation which would only be a fraud.[50] The 'perfect reader' — present in the text as the late Mr. Shawn ('so I write about the dead for the dead,' she observes, 'but I keep writing' MB 198) — reads not what he wants to hear but also things he does not like (MB 197); likewise, we may not like to read that 'all of us face impending death' (MB 102), but in the face of this reality Kincaid demostrates that it is necessary to narrate, even though writing at times must be 'about the dead for the dead.' Like a tune played by the Carib Indians' flute, Kincaid invites the audience to fill its void in unexpected ways and produce a music that results from the collaboration, not from the fragmentation and annihilation of I and You.[51] She subverts and expands our epistemological and ontological boundaries by grounds existence in birth, in the mother's womb, rather that in an impossible transcendental struggle against death and by fully accepting that subjectivity is grounded in the narrative act — and thus is, inevitably, dialogically relational. As such, it is a subjectivity which resists being inscribed as either One or Other, and its capacity to retain cultural diversity resists assimilation as well as subjugation; Kincaid's discourse insistently shows us a poetics of relating which moves beyond the personal and into the public space. As Louise Bernard argues, after Devon's death Kincaid seems to be able to mourn her brother and to bring to the foreground the silence into which the gay community in Antigua is confined.[52] This situated, embedded figuration of place and subjects prevents our reading of the Caribbean as the metaphysical space of otherness.

Mr Potter (2002)

A poetics of relating markedly characterizes the latest metamorphosis of Kincaid's prism in Mr. Potter. Subtitled 'a novel' like *The Autobiography* even though it clearly presents itself as a biography and a memoir like *My Brother, Mr. Potter* continues Kincaid's elaboration of her personal experience, her making sense of being in the world by addressing the question, 'Can a human exist in a wilderness, a world so empty of human feeling...? The answer is yes and yes again and the answer is no, not really, not so at all' (*MP* 72). The question explored by focusing on her having been brought into this world by a father who rejected his paternal responsibility and a mother who hated him. The 'novel' is thus the story of the man now dead who refused to acknowledge Kincaid's existence when she was born and who remained unknown to her. The foundational assumption of biographical narrative is radically challenged as the text repeatedly underlines that this is 'a biography of nobody' — indeed this is a meta-biography on how to turn a nobody into a somebody through writing. Explicitly and solely through her story-telling, a 'blankness,' a 'nothingness' grow into 'Mr. Potter' — into her 'father's name.' Thus it is through a speech act, or rather a writing act, that Kincaid creates Mr. Potter so that her own prismatic subjectivity can also confront the absent father-figure inexorably placed at the origin of her life; Mr. Potter exists only because he is being written on by Kincaid: in the pages of this 'novel,' his absence becomes a presence — the presence of an absent father. Therefore writing is yet again an act of telling (oneself), an endless and necessary process of auto/biography-ing which is a making sense of oneself in the attempt of making sense of the world: the prismatic subject continuously metamorphoses as she passes through life, which she attempts to change and by which she is being changed. In *Mr. Potter*, Kincaid narrates how her empowered prismatic subject can elaborate her first and most personal experience of deprivation and exclusion, and how she becomes capable of relating even to someone who has denied her existence since birth. Indeed, the prism has now grown so powerful that she can create from nothing — she can make absence present through her writing which is a 'making sense' (*MP* 181). Materialistically, writing becomes agency and thinking gives body to becoming: the making of Mr. Potter is the making sense of the prism's own being in the world when she is powerful enough to put into critical words even the blankness and nothingness that constitutes her own origin. It is significant that this

further step in the prism's empowernment is preceeded by her long
commitment to making sense of death, a making sense that allows
subjectivity to become agency without needing to be grounded on a
foundational origin.[53]

Mr. Potter is organized into twelve untitled, unnumbered chapters:
with the sole exception of chaper ten, they all start with the conjuction
'And.' This gives the narrative a breath-taking pace, underlining the
uninterrupted nature of Kincaid's writing which moves from one text
into the next in an osmotic, ever-transforming flux. This is the novel's
incipit:

> And that day, the sun was in its usual place, up above and in the middle
> of the sky, and it shone in its usual way so harshly bright, making even
> the shadows pale, making even the shadows seek shelter; that day the
> sun was in its usual place, up above and in the middle of the sky, but
> Mr. Potter did not note this, so accustomed was he to this, the sun in
> its usual place, up above and in the middle of the sky ... (*MP* 3)

Instantly, it makes us feel the unchanging tropical climate of Antigua,
so 'usual' that the same words are repeated as introduction to chapter
eight with the sole variants of: a comma before 'so harshly bright'; a
colon followed by 'and' instead of a comma after 'seeking shelter'; and a
full-stop or period instead of a semi-colon where the quotation above
ends. Most importantly, it introduces the protagonist by the juxtaposition
'but' and with a secondary negative clause: 'Mr. Potter did not note' is a
statement of his oblivion. We should consider this syntactical organization
in relation to the authorial remark placed only a few pages later in the
context of the presentation of a secondary character in the story:

> This sentence should begin with Dr. Weizenger emerging, getting off
> the launch that was brought him from his ship which is lying in the
> deep part of the harbor, but this is Mr. Potter's life and so Dr. Weizenger
> must never begin a sentence; I am not making an authorial decision, or
> a narrative decision, I only say this because this is so true: Mr. Potter's
> life is his own and no one else should take precedence. And so this
> sentence, this paragraph, will begin this way:
> When Mr. Potter first saw Dr. Weizenger ... (*MP* 8-9)

This remark calls our attention on the fact that *Mr. Potter* does not begin as it 'should' with the words 'Mr. Potter': the protagonist does not 'take precedence' but is rather subordinated, like all the other characters, to his geopolitical context; moreover, he is cast into a negative statement since his first appearance. The 'novel' is as much about him as about Antigua, 'the place which had made Mr. Potter what he was and what he would be, and all of it so without importance' (*MP* 17-18); and it is in this place, 'so without importance ... an island so small that only the very poor or the very rich could afford to live on it' (*MP* 185), that he is and will remain one who does not note. Importance and consciousness are denied to the colonized. Mr. Potter exists in 'blankness' (*MP* 9) precisely because he is incapable of relating to his own world and to the people in it, including his own numerous daughters, and of turning his own existential experience into cognition because he cannot 'read and write.' Indeed, Mr. Potter might be considered the representation of the 'small place' he inhabits, a cultural space so relentlessly and overwhelmingly marked by stories of 'displacements' that the ultimate political and philosophical significance of *Mr. Potter* is its articulation of colonialism as a thick network of displacements.

The narration produces an effect of displacement also on the readers: surrounded by the proliferation of 'And', which begin all but one chapter, a striking majority of paragraphs, and numerous sentences, we are disoriented as to where and when the story begins, develops and ends. This way we partake of the unbelonging characteristic of all the people in Mr. Potter's Antigua, people who 'all they had ever known was completely shattered and then vanished and so they had to begin again, re-create their own selves, make something new, but they couldn't do that at all' (*MP* 194). We partake of Mr. Shoul 'from the Lebanon or Syria,' an 'immigrant,' a 'person without a real home' (*MP* 110) who lived with women 'in no way related to him' (*MP* 6); of Dr. Weizenger from Prague, who could not give an accurate account of himself' because that might 'overwhelm him' and who speaks either another language or English 'as if he was in pain' (*MP* 134); of his English wife and nurse, May — the lady 'from the British Empire' (*MP* 11) who speaks an English Mr. Potter does not understand, and who calls her husband Zoltan instead of Samuel, which is the name he bore as a boy when he was 'at peace of being himself' (*MP* 31); of Mr. and Mistress Shepherd, 'both descended from African slaves' (*MP* 85), to whom Mr. Potter 'was given away' when 'his mother grew tired of him' (*MP* 70), and from whom he learned only 'cruelty, ugliness, silence, indifference' (*MP* 93); of Mr. Hall, who 'knew himself so little that when he spoke his very words seemed an approximation of what he meant to say, and all he meant to say was often false, for Mr. Hall was descended from generations of the triumphant' (*MP* 90).

Significantly, we partake also of Mr. Potter's father, Nathaniel Potter, whose life, like that of his unacknowledged son, would be 'unimaginable without that water, that land, that sky' (*MP* 37). His ancestors were 'from some of the many places that make up Africa and from somewhere in Spain and from somewhere in England and from somewhere in Scotland. And the faint sound of all that he was made of caused him to grow angry' (*MP* 39). He only 'knew eleven' of his 'twenty-one children who had different mothers' (*MP* 38) and 'greeted Mr. Potter's arrival in the world not with a feeling of happiness or feeling of unhappiness ... not even with indifference. Nathaniel Potter witheld himself from the world of Mr. Potter, my father' (*MP* 36). Of equal significance is the invitation to sympathize with Mr. Potter's mother, Elfrieda Robinson, a motherless girl of sixteen, for whom Mr. Potter's 'appearance into the world had no real meaning' (*MP* 64) and who gave him a name 'that had no meaning at all to her' (*MP* 64) and then, when he was 'five or so ... walked into the sea' (*MP* 70) 'without even so much as despair ... so much as a sense of hopelessness' (*MP* 71), thus leaving also her son motherless. Mr. Potter's absence as a father must be led back to the absence of a father and a mother in his own life, to the lack of love in his own life. Indeed the lack of love he suffered is so extreme that he himself is only capable of loving his small motorcar (*MP* 90) and a son who is not his own (his father is a fashionable undertaker), and who 'did nothing that mattered' (*MP* 159), did not even attend Mr. Potter's funeral, and died in Canada at 46; clearly, Mr. Potter loves rather the idea of having a male child rather than the person himself.

Most importantly, we are synchronized with Mr. Potter's deprivation. His displacement is the most absolute, since

> he did not own himself, he had no private thoughts, he had no thoughts of wonder, he did not have a mind's eye in which he could wander, he had no thoughts about his past, his future, and his present which lay in between them — both-his past and his future — and he was not ignorant, he was not without a conscience, he could not read and he

could not write and he could not render the story of life, his own in particular, with coherency' (*MP* 130).

Like him, we are isolated in the midst of a big ocean, we experience being physically in 'a small place' surrounded on all sides by long, successive, and never-ending waves, which bring story after story of displacement. And amidst these various stories of displacement, in the ocean of their oppressing repetitions with slight variations, stands Mr. Potter — 'a chaffeur' with 'very black skin' (*MP* 4) at the mercy of the waves, most of them similar but some unpredictably violent and others hiding a dangerous undertow, all of them mysterious in their coming and going. Here Mr. Potter is dispossessed of the articulation of his own knowledge, deprived of the possibility of making sense of his own existence, and very little else than the sounds 'eh, eh' are heard though his voice — 'Mr. Potter himself says nothing, nothing at all' (*MP* 189) underlines Kincaid in the last chapter. These sounds reproduce the repetitive, endless series of waves represented by the proliferation of 'And ...,' 'And ...,' 'And ...' in the narration; the pattern is unexpectledly interrupted by the single unpredictable 'Oh'-sounding freak wave in Chapter Ten, which provides a pause of relief, an occasion for breathing, in the obsessively syncopated music that characterizes the narration. Immersed in this ragtime-like sound, we read of a world populated by characters deprived of their place of origin and gathered in 'a very small island, an island of no account at all' (*MP* 73), where communication and relation are precluded: 'Such a dead man thought Mr. Potter to himself .... Such stupidity, thought Mr. Weizenger to himself' (*MP* 10). These different people have in common a single thing: their having come to 'a small place' from waves of displacement across the ocean, whose sound increasingly obsesses readers. The freak wave in Chapter Ten is Mr. Potter's only appearance in Kincaid's life: she was thirty-three and living in New York and he went to her house: 'his appearance was like his absence, leaving my surface untroubled, causing not so much as the tiniest ripple, leaving only an empty space inside that is small when I am not aware of its presence and large when I am' (*MP* 170). All he can tell his daughter during his visit is that her 'nose was his' and that all 'his female offspring could be identified through their noses being similar to his own' (*MP* 168); then he leaves 'forever' (*MP* 170). Even this 'Oh' remains insignificant in the economy of the novel: Mr. Potter's living never makes a difference, and the end of his life rushes to engulf him, 'like a predictable wave in a known ocean' (*MP* 194). This is so because Mr. Potter unequivocally represents colonialism: in fact, his 'lifetime began in the year fourteen hundred and ninety-two' (*MP* 177).

Possibly even more significantly, our displacement is syntonized with that of Kincaid's mother, who contrasts Mr. Potter by dominating — as it were, from behind the scene — the whole story with her defiant presence. Annie Victoria Richardson first appears briefly in Chapter One, where we read that Mr. Potter 'had not yet abandoned my mother when I was seven months old in her womb, my mother had not yet taken all his savings, money he kept in the mattress of the bed they shared together, and run away from him' (*MP* 20). Clearly, she is the one who pushes the action on, even though her appearance remains very discreet, almost imperceptible, in the first eight chapters. Nevertheless, her presence is always determinant, as in the passage reporting her failure to teach her daughter how to swim (*MP* 75), a relevant episode already in *Annie John* and a biographical detail which is here intellectually elaborated to provide a connection between Kincaid and her paternal grandmother:[54] in fact, Annie Richardson's failure to teach her daughter how to swim takes place at Rat Island, exactly where Elfrieda Robinson had drowned. Thus Kincaid first articulates her relation to her paternal grandmother, her belonging to her father's line, through a narration which conjugates the action of her mother with that of her grandmother: the former 'would take [her] to Rat Island to teach [her] how to swim' (*MP* 75), while the latter 'walked without purpose toward the sea' (*MP* 74), 'toward Rat Island' (*MP* 75). By repeatedly naming the place they share, Rat Island, and by juxtaposing their different but equally strong determination — Annie's directed defiantly against the others, Elfrieda's destructively at herself — Kincaid makes sense of both women and of her own relation to them. Only later in the narrative will she tell us also that the connection between herself and Elfrieda is biologically visible, that the shape of the nose she inherited from Mr. Potter is 'identical' to Elfieda's and 'all the girl children he fathered' (*MP* 145). But she would not tell this without making clear that a biological mark alone should not be considered significant. In fact, by observing that all the people who 'gathered around [Mr. Potter's] grave' at his funeral 'quarreled over his love, for they had nothing to show for it but their noses' (*MP* 181), she emphasizes that experience alone, unless it is culturally elaborated, does not translate into cognition.

In Kincaid's Antigua the ability for such elaboration is derived from her mother.

Precisely because Annie Richardson gives Kincaid 'the words to say it,' she imposes her presence upon the whole story, not only on Chapters Eight and Nine, which are mostly dedicated to her: 'my entire life as I live it is all my mother has told me' (*MP* 127), explains Kincaid. The narration is interspersed with phrases such as 'I know this through my mother's words,' and 'all this my mother has told me' to indicate Annie as the source of Kincaid's knowledge. Like *The Autobiography, Mr. Potter* is a truthful rather than a factual narrative — it is rooted in words. The referential reality of this realistic account, which is in all respects an auto/biography, consists of stories about its characters rather than the people themselves — its materiality is constituted by language but not for this reason is it less material. In a world in which all characters seem deprived of agency, Kincaid's mother sticks out as a powerful figure: 'she spoke English and French and a language that combined the two and she felt herself free and without boundaries' (*MP* 135). Unlike Mr. Potter, Annie Richardson 'could read and write' (*MP* 139); indeed, she owes this to her own father, who had sent her to school (see *MP* 133). And yet, it is 'against her father's wishes' that she moved 'from Dominica to Antigua when she was sixteen yeas of age' (*MP* 137). Kincaid's mother is a woman of 'formidable will, anger, and imagination' (*MP* 148), constantly presented as somenone who dominates all circumstances: things always happen to her because of her own choice and they inevitably develop into a sign of her independence. For example, she is fatherless like Mr. Potter and Kincaid herself, but this is the result of her own doing, not of her father's indifference: 'she left her home after a quarrel with her father over the way she should pursue her unfolding future, and after that quarrel, he made her dead in the realm of his fatherly love, he disinherited her' (*MP* 131). Even Mr. Potter's rejection of his fatherly responsibility is apparently triggered by Annie Richardson's action: when she 'was seven months pregnant with me, she took all of Mr. Potter's savings ... and went to live all by herself' (*MP* 142). Kincaid defines this 'a murderous action directed at [Mr. Potter], taking the money he had saved, with which he meant to make of himself some semblance of a man' and presents 'her leaving him' as the cause of 'Mr. Potter's never seeing my face when I was newly born or anytime soon after, and led to my having a line drawn through me, the space where Mr. Potter's name ought to be is not full with my father and his name, it is not empty either, it only has a line drawn through it, and that line is drawn through me' (*MP* 142-3). The absent father, responsible for 'the line drawn through,' is always a product of circumstances he does not determine; on the contrary, the powerful mother is always the force behind all events.

Even as she fails, Annie displays her formidable command, contrasted with Mr. Potter who has 'command' only over 'a small motorcar' (*MP* 89). When Kincaid was forty-one and already mother of two, her mother told her that she had tried to abort her, and this is her comment: 'she failed and that failure was because of me' (*MP* 136). Annie is thus responsible for passing on to her daughter a line of hatred, while all Mr. Potter passed on to her was a line drawn through her name, silence and indifference. Kincaid rejects both lines by refusing her name altogether: with a new name, she claims, the father's line 'could no longer find' her (*MP* 143) and by abandoning the name her mother gave her, she abandonds the line of hatred. In fact, Annie had named her 'Elaine, after a daughter of Mr. Shoul's,' because she 'had loved Mr.Shoul's chaffeur ... Mr. Potter' (*MP* 147). Soon after, though, she had 'driven a sharp knife into the heart of Mr. Potter,' thus giving birth to another line: 'this line was drawn between me and Mr. Potter and that line was firm and for our whole lives it remained unbreacheable and love could not touch it, for hatred and indifference were its name' (*MP* 148).

However, such determination is not boundless; it is limited by her daughter whom Annie does empower but cannot control. Kincaid 'came from the female line and belonged to [her] mother and to [her] mother only' (*MP* 161), and it was her mother who had taught her how to read, which 'lead to [her] knowing how to write' (*MP* 193). Her mother's teaching was even a weapon against her absent father: 'a dagger, so to speak, directed at Mr. Potter, for he lived his life deliberately ignorant of [her] existence' (*MP* 193) and did not know how 'to read and write.' Nevertheless, Annie cannot direct Kincaid, who states: 'I could not be expelled from my mother's womb at her own will' (*MP* 136). Thus, even though the engine of the entire novel is undeniably Annie — it is her 'failure' which generates the author — engines do not run on their own power. Only Kincaid herself is both powerful and in control, because she fully understands the connection and difference between reading and writing. Annie 'could read and write,' which made her more powerful than Mr. Potter, made her 'flames in her own fire' and 'an ocean with its unpredictable waves and undertow' (*MP* 135), but she 'did not think that the one had to do with the other' (*MP* 139), which made her less in command than Kincaid. In fact, the latter not only can 'read and write,' but also can tell herself 'of Mr. Potter in the written word' (*MP* 136); she 'can see' Annie and Potter as 'specters, possibilities of the real' (*MP* 137); and thus she can conjugate agency with cognition, because she writes in the attempt to 'to explain' life and to 'make sense' of it (*MP* 186).

In *My Brother* she declares: 'I became a writer out of desperation.' Yet, her writing is not an expression of despair — it is rather the cultural and political elaboration of deprivation and destitution. *Mr. Potter* further emphasizes that her writing restitutes their voice to the dispossessed, to the ancestors of slaves (*MP* 177) living in 'a small place,' and expresses their silenced knowledge of the world through relation: it is because '[her] father's absence will forever hang over [her] present, and [her] present, at any given moment, will echo his absence' (*MP* 192), that Mr. Potter's life becomes 'known, his smallness becomes large, his anonymity is stripped away, his silence broken' (*MP* 189). Kincaid breaks his silence by plunging herself into his world and bringing us along. Her lyrical narration is not the writing of an informer who 'makes' the subaltern speak. Her risk-taking storytelling — indeed, for her 'writing is a revelation'[55] — with its insistence on the interconnectedness among history, myth and poetry, redefines and reconstructs 'the interplay of lyric and narrative' imposing itself as a 'precondition of agency.'[56] Between the time of history and the time of actuality there is perfect harmony, a balanced alternation between different realities. It is in a Harrisonian 'epic voice of arrival' that she expresses the 'mixture of truth and invention' advocated in *The Autobiography*, a discursive elaboration of personal experience into political, theoretical knowledge that questions the separation between fact and fiction, self and other, language and reality. Through this storytelling the unknown and 'dull and ugly' (*MP* 88) Mr. Potter acquires a body and sense; together with the other characters, the actions, the context of the novel and most importantly the author-narrator, he gives us history which speaks to the present and points at the future to claim change.

This discourse is a silence-breaking which is a Morrisonian act of re-memorying. Knowing one's parents at the time preceeding our birth 'does seem an impossibility' (*MP* 137); yet it does materialize in this novel: 'I have in my mind a memory of them from before the time they became my mother and my father' (*MP* 137). Writing which is so compellingly storytelling makes memory possible even when there is none — no memory of Nathaniel whose life came to him 'without a reference' (*MP* 42); of Elfrieda who 'walked without purpose towards the sea' (*MP* 74); of Mr. Potter, who was 'kept from view and kept from memory' (*MP* 88). Kincaid's invocation 'Oh, memory so fresh, memory so not! Oh memory so reliable, so not! (*MP* 42) is an epic call to her muse to summon presence out of absence. 'Hear ... Hear ... Hear' (*MP* 194) is the repeated exhortation closing her telling, and undoubtedly this is a chant we have predominantly comprehended through hearing, by listening to the ragtime music produced by the rising of tunes, similar but never alike, encompassing Kincaid's revelatory making sense. We literally hear the sound of the break on the shores of a small place and we can see all the people brought here by the ocean, and even learn to understand 'the ordinarily degraded' (*MP* 80), because at work in this text is 'memory as it summons up the past, memory as it shapes the present, memory as it dictates the future' (*HG*, 218-9).

As Kincaid's writing displays its revelation, we come to see, know, and comprehend 'dull and ugly' (*MP* 88) Mr. Potter, who 'did not know about his father Nathaniel Potter' (*MP* 56) and 'could not remember his mother's name' (*MP* 84); we come to see the significance of one 'not yet in possession of the knowledge of his own misery, never to be in possession of the knowledge that the world has rained down on him injustice upon injustice, cruelty upon cruelty, never to be in possession of the knowledge that though his very being was holy, his existence was a triumph of evil' (*MP* 80). We come to note also that the author of *My Garden* associates Mr. Potter and his unknown father with plants that indicate how colonial empires affected a globalization not only of the people — Nathaniel's ancestors came 'from some of the many places that make up Africa and from somewhere in Spain and from somewhere in England and from somewhere in Scotland' (*MP* 39) — but also of the landscape in 'a small place.' In fact, Nathaniel is affiliated to a tamarind tree, 'native to tropical Asia' (*MP* 98), and Mr. Potter to 'a wormwood' and a *Tradescantia albiflora* (*MP* 53), the former a bitter shrub used as a vermifuge, the *absinthium* of the Old World, and the latter a noxious, invasive weed from South America, cultivated as a houseplant and known by the common name 'wandering jew' — itself a symbol of displacement. We come to grasp the meaning of naming by observing how this man who was 'not an original man,' because 'he was not made from words' (*MP* 55) is related to his names: Elfrieda named him Rodney 'after the English maritime criminal George Brydges Rodney' (*MP* 63-4) but called him Roderick because 'she wanted a name that had no meaning at all to her' (*MP* 64); then the others called him Drickie (*MP* 64) and he later 'came to call himself Mr. Potter to anyone who wanted to be chaffeured' (*MP* 89). We learn why Jamaica Kincaid 'first abandoned and then changed' her name — 'Elaine Cynthia Potter, crossed out by the line that was drawn through it' (*MP* 143) and also to notice that her mother's last name, Richardson, is omitted in this version of the story. We pay attention to Dr. Weizenger's name changing from Samuel to Zoltan (*MP* 33), and we notice the careless indication 'from the Lebanon or Syria, some place like that' (*MP* 6) after Mr. Shoul's name. As we develop a sharp eye for the significance of naming, not only do we remember the strict association between naming and possessing in 'Ovando' and 'On Seeing England for the First Time' and see how the lack of understanding this equation for the people inhabiting 'a small place' is yet another sign of their misery, but we also recognize that the repeated attention to naming is related to the focus of the story: Kincaid writes Mr. Potter because 'Potter' is in her name and because the line drawn through that name on her birth certificate left an empty space (*MP* 100) that only her writing can fill. The intimate relationship between narrator and story produces the lyrical and epic voice characteristic of her discourse. In the process of telling, Kincaid herself is 'metamorphosed into something new' (*MP* 154): her prismatic subjectivity not only changes the light passing through her but is also constantly changed by it. The first light that hit her prism was her mother's. Thanks to her rage and hatred, to her violence and unpredictale fury, and mostly thanks to her words, memory can be reconstructed and even created — thinking can be rethought. The 'female line' of hatred (*MP* 164) produces the means to fill the blank left by the male line of indifference. The 'cruelty and ugliness' of colonialism, the 'silence and indifference' (*MP* 92) it produced can be filled and broken to express the world it censored, 'the world as it is made up of that great big thing: a shared commonality, feelings of love for something ordinary, like his own child regardless of the shape of their nose' (*MP* 172). Annie giving her daughter 'the words to say it' is the necessary, empowering anticolonial voice, speaking against, rejecting, and defying the other; Kincaid, acknowledging her mother's words and digging out other words from the immense silence of 'a small place' is the postcolonial voice, speaking for and with the silenced, in the effort to change not only the world but also our thinking about it — a change thus defined by the difficult alliance between performance and cognition.

Precisely this alliance brings to my mind Barbara Johnson's sharp reading of Melville's *Billy Budd,* where she observes that 'to repeat is to be ungovernably open to revision, displacement, and reversal.'[57] Certainly the multiplication of stories about Mr. Potter echoes the propagation of tales about Billy and it likewise aims at making sense of the immense gaps in understanding the complexity of 'a small place.' Surely the roles Johnson attributes to Billy, Claggart and Vere, respectively as naïve, ironic and political reader, suggest similar considerations about Mr. Potter, Annie and Kincaid. Mr. Potter's 'eh eh' recalls Billy's stutter, and so does his naïvete. Like his father, who 'was only that, Nathaniel Potter' and who 'asked himself, not a thing' (*MP* 43), Mr. Potter is also just himself, a perfect coincidence of word and thing to be taken at face value, suggesting straightforward, completely successful communication. From the beginning we read that 'nothing entered his mind, his mind was already filled up with Mr. Potter' (*MP* 27), a statement reiterated in the concluding paragraph: 'Mr. Potter was my father, my father's name was Mr. Potter' (*MP* 195). Thus the scanty words we receive from this man are to be taken as a reliable indication of the cracks in his own doing and understanding.

Mr. Potter's simplicity and transparency contrasts Annie's ambiguity: her relation to language is ironic, like Claggart's. Her words are always a reaction, a response to other words, the outcome of violent quarrels with her father; she is the unexpected wave in the ocean, the undertow in the water; her words are askew, never to be taken at face value. For example, Kincaid reports what her mother told her about weaning her ('what she said to me') and then adds, 'my mother said that she did not remember telling me,' adding that the episode, 'could not have happened since she could not remember it happening so' (*MP* 144). Clearly her words are more 'truthful' than 'factual' and they always require interpretation. Witness, for instance, the statement 'I never knew his face' (*MP* 104), referring to Mr. Potter, corrected later by the more complex statement: 'when I was about four years old, I saw Mr. Potter ... that time I waved to Mr. Potter, for I could see his face (or I could see what I thought was his face, though I never saw his face at all, not then, not later when he was standing in front of me)' (*MP* 125), and further on by the specification, 'I remember this incident of waving to him because my mother has told me about it and through my mother's words, I have come to see myself waving to Mr. Potter' (*MP* 126), reiterated by 'And all this is what my mother has told me' (*MP* 127). Annie's ambiguities are as strong a call for interpretation as are Mr. Potter's gaps and this role is taken on by Kincaid.

Like Captain Vere, Kincaid is the political reader, capable of conjugating action and language, of working on the relation between paranoia and naivete, of producing complexity and accepting contingency. Like the Captain, she condemns both by stating that she wishes them both dead and indeed at the time of her writing they are both dead, thus transforming their violence into her authority. Unlike the narrator in 'Ovando,' her understanding is not without judgement: she understands Potter's transparency and socially explains his limitations as much as she understands Annie's rage and hatred and rejects these aspects of the only line of belonging she claims her own. Her judgement derives from a queer look at the complexity of 'a small place,' a gaze capable of juggling infinite contradictions because it is capable of mainatining an askew, indirect, relational position as it makes sense of the immense unknown spaces which open up between knowing and doing, between cognition and performance, as it elaborates the discontinuities created by Mr. Potter's silences and Annie's proclamations to embrace in its dialogical understanding the beautiful 'shared commonality, feeling of love for something ordinary' (*MP* 172) that the world should be.

Kincaid's reading in *Mr. Potter* is thus a queer reading of 'a small place'; as such it produces writing which is as beautiful as Kincaid's mother was before she started the line of hatred ('how beautiful she was then' *MP* 132; 'she was very beautiful' *MP* 135) and even as beautiful as Mr. Potter might have been sometimes because 'often a thing that is ugly is not only a definition of beauty itself but also renders beauty as something beyond words or beyond any kind of description' (*MP* 88). Elaine Scarry's clever discussion of the political and philosophical significance of beauty encourages me to insist on the beauty of Kincaid's writing. Scarry observes that beauty is 'life-granting':[58] *Mr. Potter* gives life not only to Kincaid's absent father but also to her capacity to relate to him; Scarry further notes that beauty is 'unself-interested' (119): *Mr. Potter* is unquestionably focused on making sense of the colonization of minds rather than on the

story of Kincaid's own family. Scarry also points out that beauty is
characterized by a 'forward momentum ... a desire to bring new things
onto the world' (46), which is also a desire to carry greetings from other
worlds' (47): *Mr. Potter* like all of Kincaid's works has carried greetings of
voices 'from other worlds' to us. Indeed, what is beautiful is as fair as
what is just and aesthetic symmetry runs parallel to social equality —
relentlessly and always more compellingly Kincaid's works bring to us
words of justice that are also words of beauty.[59] It could not be otherwise,
since such words are articulated by the prismatic subject who, 'many-
sided and transparent, refracting and reflecting light,' became so 'beautiful'
(*BR* 80).

Notes

1   For a detailed biography of Kincaid, see Lizabeth Paravisini-Gebert, *Jamaica Kincaid: A Critical Companion*, Westport, CT: Greenwood P, 1999:1-23.

2   Jamaica Kincaid with Dwight Garner, Interview, *Salon Magazine*, 13 January, 1996, located at http://www.salon1999.com/05/features/kincaid.html (01/05/98)

3   The images of the Caribbean as land undifferentiated from sea, crossroad, repeating island, dissemi/nation, Black Atlantic People, space of liminality, New World Mediterranean, and so on, are of course related to formulations that are neither reductionist nor romantically seductive (see, for example, Edouard Glissant, *Caribbean Discourse*, Charlottesville: University Press of Virginia, 1989; Homi Bhabha, 'DissemiNation: time, narrative, and the margins of the modern mation' in *Nation and Narration*, London: Routledge, 1990: 291-232; Antonio Benìtez-Rojo, *The Repeating Island*, Durham: Duke University Press, 1992; Paul Gilroy, *The Black Atlantic*, Cambridge: Harvard UP, 1993; Michael Dash, *The Other America*, Charlottesville: UP of Virginia, 1998). The risk is that it is only the icons that are set into discursive circulation, thus confining the Caribbean again to its colonial space of otherness. The Caribbean has been cited as the most challenging area for postcolonial studies (see Bill Ashcroft, Gareth Griffiths, and Helen Tiffin, *The Empire Writes Back*, London: Routledge, 1989): I think the overwhelmingly intricate and long history of misrepresentation it has been subjected to as the grounding locus of otherness makes it resistant to representation and for this reason historically grounded and politically contextualized figurations are most useful for breaking the silence into which it has been confined. Michael Dash offers a definition of Caribbean literature as a 'multiple series of literary relations' (p. 20). Jamaica Kincaid's inquiry into the gendered social and ethic implications of a poetics of relation in my view fully accounts for her Caribbeanness.

4   Too often the Caribbean and the idea of creolization have been reduced to a facile postmodernist gesture in which anything goes. The seduction of this easy solution is wiped off by any glance at the socio-political reality of a region in which, for example, the incidence of AIDS is second only to that of sub-Saharian Africa.

5   M. Nourbese Philip, *A Genealogy of Resistance*, Toronto: Mercury P, 1997, p.67.

6   Jamaica Kincaid with Kay Bonetti, Interview, *Missouri Review*, located at http://webdelsol.com/Missouri Review/interviews/kincaid.html (01/05/98).

7   Angela Carter, 'Notes from the Frontline,' in Michelène Wandor, ed., *On Gender and Writing*, London: Pandora, 1983: 69-77, and Edward Said, *Culture and Imperialism*, New York: Vintage, 1993.

8   The Workshop 'Travelling Concepts' of the European Thematic Network Athena2, directed by Rosi Braidotti, is currently interrogating these concepts to research the transmission of knowledge and practice across cultures and the development of a transnational ethics and pedagogy of complexity and ambiguity.

9   Wilson Harris, 'Quetzalcoatl and the Smoking Mirror (Reflections on Originality and Tradition)' (Address to Temenos Academy, London, 7 February 1994), *The Review of Contemporary Fiction*, 17:2 (Summer 1997): 12-23.

10   Adriana Cavarero, *Tu che mi guardi, tu che mi racconti. Filosofia della narrazione*, Milano: Feltrinelli, 1997.

11   Gayatri C. Spivak, *Outside in the Teaching Machine*, New York: Routledge, 1993, p. 15.

12   See Adrienne Rich, *What is Found There, Notebooks on Poetry and Politics*, New York: Norton, 1993; Liana Borghi, 'Introduzione: L'occhio del[l]'ago' in *Passaggi: Letterature comparate al femminile*, Urbino: Quattroventi, 2002; Toni Morrison, *Playing in the Dark*, New York: Vintage, 1992.

13   An earlier version of this section appeared as 'Re-memorying, Decolonising and Translating in Jamaica Kincaid's *The Autobiography of My Mother*' in Joan Anim-Addo, ed., *The Centre of Remembrance*, London: Mango Publishing, 2002: 52-65.

14   Gayatri C. Spivak, 'The Politics of Translation' in Michèle Barrett and Anne Phillips, eds., *Destabilizing Theory: Contemporary Feminist Debates*, Palo Alto, CA: Stanford UP, 1992: 177-200, p. 192.

15   Jamaica Kincaid with Allan Vorda, Interview, *The Mississippi Review*, 2:4 (April 1996), located at http://sushi.st.usm.edu/mrw/9604/kincaid.html. (01/05/98).

16   Respectively, from the following: Felicia Lee, 'A Writer Who Illuminates Her Own Dark Words' Rev. of *The Autobiography of My Mother: A Novel* in *New York Times*; Thursday, Jan. 25, 1996: B1; Eavan Boland, 'Desolation Angel' Rev. of *The Autobiography of My Mother: A Novel*, in *Voice Literary Supplement*, Feb. 1996: 11; Richard Eder, Rev. of *The Autobiography of My Mother: A Novel,* in *Newsday*, Jan. 14, 1996, located at: http://www.newsday.com/books/bkautobi.htm (01/05/98); Elizabeth Manus, Rev. of *My Brother* in *Boston Phoenix*, Oct. 20, 1997, located at <http//weeklywire.com/ww/10-20-97/boston_books_1.htlm> (01/05/98); Cathleen Schine, 'A World as Cruel as Job's' Rev. of *The Autobiography of My Mother: A Novel* in *New York Times Book Review*, February 4, 1996: 5; and Richard Eder, Rev. of *The Autobiography of My Mother*.

17   See Felicia Lee, 'A Writer Who Illuminates Her Own Dark Words' and Steve Horowitz, Rev. of *The Autobiography of My Mother: A Novel* in *Icon (Iowa City)*, February 8, 1996, located at: http://www.iowacity.com/icon/backs/1996/02-08-96/books.htm (01/05/98)

18   Jamaica Kincaid with Eleanor Wachtel, Interview, *Malahat Review*, vol. 116(Fall 1996): 55-71.

19   See Jamaica Kincaid with Marilyn Snell, 'Jamaica Kincaid Hates Happy Endings' Interview in *Mother Jones*, Sept./Oct. 1997, located at: <http:// www.mojones.com/ mother_jones/SO97/snell.html> (01/05/98).

20   See Lennard Davis, *Factual Fictions: The Origins of the English Novel*, Philadelphia: University of Pennsylvania Press, 1983.

21   Rikki Ducornet, *The Monstrous and the Marvelous*, San Francisco: City Lights, 1999, p. 115.

22   Rikki Ducornet, *The Monstrous and the Marvelous*, p. 116p.

23   Marianne Cook, *Generations of Women: In Their Own Words*, San Francisco: Chronicle Books, 1998, p. 20.

24   See Sidonie Smith, *A Poetics of Women's Autobiography: Marginality and the Fictions of Self-Representation*, Bloomington: Indiana University Press, 1987; Luce Irigaray, in *Ethique de la difference sexuelle*, Paris: Minuit, 1985; Judith Butler, *Bodies that Matter: On the Discursive Limits of 'Sex'*, London: Routledge, 1993; Lorna Goodison, *I Am Becoming My Mother*, London: New Beacon, 1986.

25   On the articulation of feminst subjectivity as metamorphosis, see Rosi Braidotti, *Metamorphoses: Towards a Materialist Theory of Becoming*, Cambridge, UK: Polity Press, 2002. Braidotti's emphasis on historical specificity, ethical concerns, transformative embedded figurations and sexual difference is in tune with the transformations of Kincaid's prismatic subjectivity through her subsequent stories.

26   Jamaica Kincaid with Kay Bonetti, Interview, *Missouri Review*, located at http:// webdelsol.com/Missouri Review/interviews/kincaid.html (01/05/98); Jamaica Kincaid with Dwight Garner, Interview, *Salon Magazine*, January 13, 1996; Jamaica Kincaid with with Allan Vorda, Interview, *The Mississippi Review*, 2:4 (April 1996; and Jamaica Kincaid with Eleanor Wachte, Interview, *Malahat Review*, vol. 116 (Fall 1996).

27   See Kathryn E. Morris, 'Jamaica Kincaid's Voracious Bodies: Engendering a Carib(bean) Woman,' *Callaloo* 25.3 (2002): 954-68 and Gary E. Holcomb and Kimberly S. Holcomb, 'I Made Him: Sadomasochism in Kincaid's *The Autobiography of My Mother*,' *Callaloo* 25.3 (2002): 969-76. Morris notices that S/M does not link power to fate or nature but rather considers it a social, conventional performance; therefore, she argues, Xuela's narcissistic and frightening sexuality may be symbolically considered as the expression of a transgressive relationship and, she concludes, 'through the renounciation of motherhood, her narcissistic sexuality and the strength of her imagination ... Xuela emerges as a fictional response to the historically objectified Carib woman and the Carib/cannibal myth' (p. 966).The Holcombs focus their reading on S/M theory and its intersection with colonialism and observe that in the sex act between Xuela and Phillip (*A* 154-5) Xuela simulates a reversal of colonial power and dominates Phillip thus shifting agency from the master's to the slave's body and blurring the distinction between the two.

28   Jamaica Kincaid with Eleanor Wachtel, Interview.

29   Diane Simmons, 'Loving Too Much' in Alfred Horning et al., eds., *Postcolonialism and Autobiography*, Amsterdam: Rodopi, 1998: 233-245, p.244.

30   Isabel Hoving, In *Praise of New Travelers: Reading Caribbean Migrant Women's Writing*, Stanford, CA: Stanford University Press, 2001, pp. 224, 236.

31   Laura Niesen de Abruna, 'Jamaica Kincaid's Writing and the Maternal-Colonial
      Matrix' in Mary Condé and Thorunn Lonsdale, eds., *Caribbean Women Writers:
      Fiction in English*, New York: St. Martin's, 1999:172-183.

32   Alison Donnell, 'When Writing the Other is Being True to the Self' in Pauline
      Polkey, ed.; *Women's Lives into Print*, New York: S. Martin's, 1999: 123-135, pp.
      134, 135.

33   K.T. Mcguire, Rev. of *The Autobiography of My Mother: A Novel* located at: http://
      www.desires.com/2.1/Word.Reviews/Docs/kincaid.html (01/05/98); and Tai
      Moses, 'A Motherless Child Rages in Jamaica Kincaid's Searing 'Autobiography''
      Rev. of *The Autobiography of My Mother: A Novel* in *Metro*, Feb. 15-21, 1996, located
      at: http://www.metroactive.com/papers/metro/02.15.96/kincaid-9607.html (01/
      05/98).

34   Edouard Glissant, *Caribbean Discourse*, Charlottesville: University Press of Virginia,
      1989, p. 141.

35   In this I must depart from Lizabeth Paravisini-Gebert, *Jamaica Kincaid: A Critical
      Companion*, Westport, CT: Greenwood Press, 1999, who declares: 'Xuela has no
      interest in political activity .... She remains to the end obsessed by the past, unable
      — unwilling perhaps — to look beyond her anger to a future of transcendence
      through violent revolution, prompting instead the question whether the societies
      of the Caribbean, like Xuela, are damaged beyond repair' (p.163). Rather, I would
      emphasize with Alexandra Schultheis, 'Family Matters in Jamaica Kincaid's *The
      Autobiography of My Mother*' located at <http://social.class.ncsu.edu/jouvert/v5i2/
      kincai/htm> (21-Jan-02) that Xuela produces 'identities of subject and motion
      that are feminized but not necessarily maternal, representative but not totalizing'
      and that refuse any 'nostalgic return to coherent subjectivity, essential gender
      and racial identifications, or firm national identity' (p. 13).

36   Figurations articulated respectively by Michael Dash, *The Other America* and
      Edouard Glissant, *Caribbean Discourse*.

37   Rhonda Cobham, 'Mwen Na Rien, Msieu': Jamaica Kincaid and the Problem of
      Creole Gnosis' in *Callaloo* 25:3 (Summer 2002): 868-884, p. 881.

38   Wilson Harrís, 'Quetzalcoatl and the Smoking Mirror (Reflections on Originality
      and Tradition)' (Address to Temenos Academy, London, 7 February 1994), *Review
      of Contemporary Fiction*, 17:2 (Summer 1997): 12-23.

39   Adriana Cavarero, *Tu che mi guardi, tu che mi racconti. Filosofia della narrazione*,
      Milano: Feltrinelli, 1997.

40   Sarah Brophy, 'Angels in Antigua: The Diasporic of Melancholy in Jamaica Kincaid's
      My Brother' *PMLA*, March 2002: 265-77, p. 265.

41   Sarah Brophy, 'Angels in Antigua,' p. 268.

42   Sarah Brophy, 'Angels in Antigua,' p. 274.

43   Adriana Cavarero, *Tu che mi guardi, tu che mi racconti*, pp. 35-7.

44   Most likely the Author herself, as Opal Palmer Adisa kindly suggested at the
      Caribbean Women Writers Conference 'Swinging Her Breasts at History' (London:
      Goldsmiths, 1998).

45   This detailed, complex metanarrative discussion of the genre of *My Brother* recalls
      the innovative genres adopted in Kincaid's previous texts and thus underlines the

impact of her writing as a whole upon our conception of narration. I believe it also negates Sangeeta Ray's interpretation in 'Ethical Encounters: Spivak, Alexander and Kincaid,' *Cultural Studies*, 17(1) 2003:42-55. Ray declares that '*My Brother* eludes generic classification. It is ostensibly a biography of Kincaid's brother who dies of AIDS in Antigua. But it is also about Kincaid herself, her inability to come to terms with her mother and her brothers, with the life she has long left behind in Antigua. ... Family to Kincaid means only the one she has formed in Vermont with her husband and two children.' According to Ray, this 'makes a her a poor reader of the narrative of her life ... a postcolonial subject turned migrant who returns to the non-metropolic and fails to read the native subject.' Ray drastically concludes that '*My Brother* best captures the narcissism of the immigrant who returns home as a transnational figure of mobility and fails to grasp the significance of transnational literacy' (p. 54).

46 Respectively from the following reviews: Elizabeth Manus, Rev. of *My Brother*; Paula Woods, Rev. of *My Brother*. located at: <http//your.accessatlanta.com/entertainment/books/jamaica_kincaid.html> (05/06/2001); Peter Kurth, '*My Brother*: A Memoir' Rev. of *My Brother* in Salon, Oct. 9, 1997, located at: http://www.salonmagazine.com/books/sneaks/1997/10/09review.html (05/06/2001); John Skow, 'Family Ties' Rev. of *The Autobiography of My Mother: A Novel* in *Time Magazine*, November 10, 1997, 150:20, located at: <http//mouth.pathfinder.com/time/magazine/1997/dom/9.../the_arts_book.family_ties_.htm> (05/06/2001); Elizabeth Manus, Rev. of *My Brother*.

47 Wilson Harris, 'Quetzalcoatl and the Smoking Mirror,' p.22.

48 Wilson Harris, 'Quetzalcoatl and the Smoking Mirror,' p. 18.

49 Elizabeth Manus, Rev. of *My Brother*; Peter Kurth, '*My Brother*: A Memoir' Rev.

50 Adriana Cavarero, *Tu che mi guardi, tu che mi racconti*, p. 126.

51 Wilson Harris, 'Cross-Cultural Crisis: Imagery, Language and the Intuitive Imagination,' Commonwealth Lectures 1990 n. 2, Oct. 31, 1990. University of Cambridge.

52 Louise Bernard, 'Countermemory and Return: Reclamation of the (Postmodern) Self in Jamaica Kincaid's *The Autobiography of My Mother* and *My Brother*' in MFS 48:1 (Spring 2002):113-138.

53. Since her earliest publications, Kincaid has been writing about death and nothingness, about leaving her mother and country and about the silence imposed upon her people and culture by colonialism and slavery. In his paper delivered at the North American Comparative Literature Association Meeting in San Juan, Puerto Rico, April 13, 2002, Thomas W. Sheenan emphasizes how *A Small Place*, *Lucy*, *The Autobiography of My Mother* and *Mr Brother* are stories of the historical lack of the Caribbean — a space which can only be addressed or recounted, and victory or revenge will not close it or heal it.

54 As confirmed also by Ian Frazier in his 'Foreword' to Jamaica Kincaid, *Talk Stories*, New York: Farrar Straus and Giroux, 2001, p. xviii.

55 Jamaica Kincaid with Allan Vorda, Interview in *The Mississippi Review*, 2:4 (April 1996).

56   Susan Stanford Friedman, *Mappings*, Princeton: Princeton University Press, 1998, p. 242.

57   Barbara Johnson, 'Melville's Fist' in *The Critical Difference*, Baltimore: Johns Hopkins University Press, 1980:79-109, p. 81.

58   Elaine Scarry, *On Beauty and Being Just*, Princeton: Princeton University Press, 1999, p. 69.

59   Elaine Scarry, *On Beauty and Being Just*, pp. 97-8.

Reprise

Prismatic Subjects Making Sense of a Globalized World

Jamaica Kincaid has kept me company since 1983: she has given me words to make sense of my own being in the world from the conjugation of feminism with postmodernism and womanism, through the affiliation of feminism with postcolonial studies, to the articulation of feminism and queer theory. Her words have successively enabled me to account for the complexity produced by the continuously shifting and increasingly disseminated forces that characterize power within the contemporary context. Through her words, the theoretical articulations that have always empowered my own making sense of being in the world have acquired a materialist consistency and have productively indicated the links with the ideas and figurations that other writers and thinkers have suggested to me. What Kincaid says about plants — 'I must say that I don't love things and then abandon them, I've kept all my loves, I only add to them'[1] — I can state about my own feminist affiliations: in my own gardening/thinking, a postmodernism of resistance still shows its sprouts among the tufts of postcolonialism, the bushes of queer theory, the trees of creolité, and is waiting for more flowers and weeds, planned and unexpected, to crowd its bed.

Kincaid also says that 'gardening is a personal thing':[2] I am deeply aware that the garden I have been making through my readings is no more than a 'personal thing,' but I nevertheless hope that it may be shared by others, since it grows out of my encounters with others, like gardening, which Kincaid also points 'is learning from one's conceitedness and mistakes as from gardeners' (MG 173). I have read Kincaid as a white European feminist educated in the US, and my readings bear the traces of my own roots and routes; my meanderings have brought me to more encounters than my memory has allowed me to acknowledge.[3] I am not a good gardener, neither literally nor metaphorically; my garden looks rather like a jungle than anything else. Nevertheless, it bears two crucial meanings: it is indissoluble from me and it has enabled me to create my own space. Through her gardening Kincaid has created a metaphorical map of the Caribbean in Vermont, thus representing her new definition of home. By comparison, when thinking about my own reading and writing in terms of a Kincaidian gardening I think I have figured exchanges and connections that bring new places into my home. The making of this private garden has provided an empowering tool for my own socio-political commitment: by showing some routes that may lead me to share with Kincaid's discursive community, it has pointed the way for envisioning the Spivakian 'internationality of ecological justice in the impossible, undivided world of which one must dream.'[4]

Conscious that my present articulation of feminism is not a point of arrival but only another passage in the continuous changing that characterizes our living — a flux so perfectly captured by Kincaid in the metaphor of the garden as always in the making (MG 7) — I would like to borrow from Dana Nelson the suggestion to 'experiment with embracing disagreement practically and emotionally in order to reorient our energy toward democracy.' Following her indication means replacing the idea of the nation with that of democracy, and the idea of 'oppositional histories' with that of 'democratic citizenship'; when it comes to the work of democracy, 'there are no clean choices there is just the risk and the mess and the temporal rewards of proliferating politicalness.'[5] Undeniably, this line of action springs from the Enlightenment idea of replacing aristocracy with democracy and thus carries the earlier legacy of colonial as well as the present burden of global territorial and cultural appropriations. It is indeed very difficult to propose the idea of democracy in the present context marked by the 'global triumph of 'America'' and to seriously hope that it will not be subsumed under the capitalist democracy that serves the present imperial project.[6]

However, once the 'impossible dream' of international ecological justice is materialistically approached, I do not see an alternative to facing what Melville aptly called the 'ragged edges' of a 'truth uncompromisingly told.' Gardening is a messy, risky, and only temporarily rewarding matter, and gardening for Kincaid entails 'making,' which means thinking by process, flux, and interconnections rather than by fixed concepts.[7] Spivak reads Kincaid's *Lucy* as an exemplary instance of parataxis and appreciates its power to withhold connections as a sign of the protagonist's withdrawal from affective connections; she interprets Lucy's 'big blur' as an indication that the text points outside selfhood towards the capacity to claim the right of 'responsibility as ability to love.'[8] Lucy's 'big blur' together with Annie's prism have made me 'stick' to Kincaid's discourse and love it in the political sense suggested by Spivak: if 'love is an effort — over which one has no control yet at which one must not strain — which is slow, attentive on both sides — how does one win the attention of the subaltern without coercion or crisis? — mindchanging on both sides,' then Lucy's painful disconnection from her mother in Antigua and critical connection with Mariah in the US have certainly enabled my translation of Lucy's cultural practices into my own effort to modify the culture I inhabit. Lucy has provided 'the mind-changing one-on-one responsible contact' without which nothing of our collective political efforts towards pursuing laws to guarantee international justice 'will stick.'[9] Her tears erasing her own name have severed her original, predetermined connection with Antigua but only to return to it over and over again in order to rewrite this beginning. The 'big blur' indicates both her sacrifice and liberation; to me it clearly indicates that Kincaid's narrators never act as native informants nor as speakers for silenced subalterns. Kincaid does not write in order to increase her readers' knowledge of the Other world; rather, Annie, Lucy, Xuela, and Kincaid herself are voices in a connected world; they variously inhabit the island in the Third World or the metropolis in the First World and articulate the world as a whole in stories that allow us all to envision ways to overcome the opposition between First and Third Worlds. Kincaid's prismatic subjects constantly deconstruct the juxtaposition between Culture and Other Cultures and uncompromisingly critique not only colonialism but also postcolonial reason.

These voices have obliged me to conceive identity as a subjectivity which is embodied power and desire and which is projected towards the construction of discursive communities, thereby embodying the ethical commitment to accept experiencing the impossible. Such construction is fragmentary, multiple, repetitive and each time situated and in process, because culture is alive only in the plural and 'on the run'; its beauty is unself-interested, relational, and always conjugated with justice.[10] From prismatic subjectivity I have learned to be content never to rest on the found, never to be satisfied with what I already know; the prism has taught me how to be nurtured by a crisscrossing of perspectives, languages, and constituencies. My feminist focus on sexual and gender difference has been nurtured over these years by postmodernist theory, deconstructive practice, womanist thought, and later by a growing familiarity with Caribbean women's literature and by postcolonial and queer theory. I have come to adopt a practice of interruption and to perform a thinking that crosses and is crossed over, that is oblique and transversal, and that accepts going wrong or misunderstanding the world in order to test new parameters of comprehension. Postcolonial concerns within feminist studies have increasingly brought me to accept locating my own thinking within a liminalien space.[11] Pragmatically, I find it fruitful to conjugate these various approaches to articulate a reading position that inhabits a space of osmotic relations and eases my understanding, on the one hand, of the increasing complexity and, on the other, of the increasing oversimplification of reality. I aim at referring materialistically to the temporality of my being in the world in order to participate in a culture capable of accounting for the economics and cultural geographies shaped by the ongoing process of globalization.

To relate these general remarks with a theoretical example related to the specific locus of the Caribbean, I'd like to conclude my reading of Kincaid with a reflection on the word *creole*. Provocatively, I want to decontextualize this concept in order to use it as a thinking exercise; instrumentally, I propose *creole* as a possible translation of the word *queer* within the context of theoretical debate. There are, of course, good reasons for making this operation anything other than a temporary heuristic device. First of all, suggesting *creole* to render *queer* is an inconsiderate act of displacement, which may rather be described as deportation, because it despoils Caribbean historical specificity.

Nevertheless, the suggestion also entails acknowledging the impossibility of rendering *queer* into other languages. Gottlieb would label as 'resignation' this translation strategy, and I like this connotated category, since taken at face value, 'resignation' underlines the failure of proposing a plausible translation — certainly *queer does not mean creole*. As an ironic gesture, however, 'resignation' in its meaning of 'solution dictated by extraneous factors' may refer to the success of a cultural exchange and mutual enrichment.[12] This appears evident to me: both *queer* and *creole* point towards a displacement, a redefinition which is never given outside of its context, a gaze which is always askew, a speaking which is always transversal and parodic.[13] Indeed, in this sense what is *creole* may also be *queer*: both terms imply a history of repression — one racial and the other sexual; both indicate what is contaminated, interrupted by something else, crossed over, interfered with; both have historically been used as offensive epithets and are now being reappropriated as empowering identity-markers; finally, both underline a fluid, temporal, relational and migrant conception of subjectivity. Since the practice of translation is culturally stimulating precisely because of its impossibility, I hope that the cultural displacements set in motion by considering this 'resignation' might prove theoretically fruitful notwithstanding their historical and political impossibility. Within a context increasingly defined by global forces, I am convinced that the efforts to give shape to a postcolonial culture, capable of supporting globalized solidarity, exchange, and coalitions among different local constituencies and of contrasting a globalization characterized instead by the domination of a few military, economic, and financial powers are more effectively pursued through acts of 'resignation' — , that is, through the impossible and yet necessary act of cultural translation. This parallels the slow, complex, and on-going task of political reconciliation, rather than the immediate revolutionary action or the momentary oppositional gesture.

Creolizing/Queering captures in unpredictable and shifting ways the relational nature of Caribbean history and culture by favouring thinking and acting which aim at surprising and blurring the boundaries among monolithic representations, and by encouraging mutual interruption. Caryl Phillips describes the Caribbean as the meeting of Europe and Africa on the American soil — the place where Europe deported Africa and slaughtered America.[14] Jack Forbes reserves the name of 'true Americans' to the people resulting from this clashing encounter, thus deconstructing racism through a detailed and complex taxonomical history of race.[15] The Caribbean is also a fluid place, Edouard Glissant reminds us, made of land and sea, a sea which divides as well as unites the differences of the various lands of the region; it is indeed 'the repeating island' described by Antonio Benìtez-Rojo.[16] It certainly is empowering to think about the Caribbean as a crossroads of many encounters, rather than as the Other World. In addition, with regard to the diaspora that has disseminated Caribbean people and their culture in so many countries of the First World, it appears increasingly also evident that the so-called First and Third Worlds are tied together by intricate and mutual relations which complicate their assumed dichotomy. If historically the Caribbean has been described as the land where languages, peoples and cultures became creolized, it is now better configured as a space inhabited by a field of relations crossing one another and being crossed over. Since the beginning of its modern history, this space has been characterized by the plural connotation of the word *creole*, meaning variably a person of mixed race, a colonist living in the colony, or the contaminated language of the colonized. *Creole* resists being anchored to a single meaning as much as Caribbean resists signifying alterity. Caribbean writers and intellectuals have powerfully destroyed the Columbian figuration of 'the otro mundo,' making it no longer tenable to think in terms of the West and the Rest, with the Caribbean troped as the exemplary Otherness of Western colonial domination, invariably raped, robbed, exploited, eroticized, and orientalized. Caribbean literature is showing us all how to begin articulating the Caribbean and consequently ourselves in postcolonial terms — as a collectivity, a community of differences, rather than a binary opposition. Jamaica Kincaid has largely contributed to my understanding of this complexity of the creolized/queered nature of Caribbean alterity, which should both be fostered and resisted.

In the first place, Kincaid's writing compels academics to creolize one dichotomy that still holds uncontested citizenship in the literary discipline: the opposition between poetry and theory. Her lyrical voice, for whom 'poetry is not a luxury,' powerfully utters a materialist theory uncompromisingly capable of accepting the temporality of being and deeply aware that no new understanding can be achieved without the creation of new words. From this position, Kincaid nicely illuminates the osmotic relationship between empires and colonies during the hegemony of the British Empire and between centres and peripheries at the time of the domination exerted by the IMF and global markets. Her (auto)biographical stories move in and out of the private and public and show globalization's rootedness in colonialism and colonial culture. They also show equally well that for the liberation forces which shattered European hegemony during the last century it became possible to participate in the Pan-Africanist movement and fruitfully bring together the Caribbean and the European metropolis, Harlem and Africa, because they were acting within a colonially globalized context. The precarious balance between the two oppositional forces, colonial and anti-colonial, is effectively addressed in *A Small Place*. Janus-faced like a 'resignation' strategy, the 'you' called into question by the narrator's first utterance is a tourist as well as a despicable colonizer, but not for this reason is the 'they' referring to the colonized left unblemished.

A 'liminalien' citizen of Antigua living in Vermont, Jamaica Kincaid inhabits a threshold cultural space, a passage that joins and separates Vermont from Antigua indicating that after modern imperialist expansion many have plural locations and citizenship needs to be redefined. She positions herself as a speaking subject who refuses autarchy, who rejects the idea that any culture can exist as a monolith, and that there is always somewhere a *heim* to escape from the uncanny, *unheimlich*, condition of temporality. In so doing, she manages to keep a critical eye on both 'the victor' and 'the vanquished,' blaming Mariah in *Lucy* for wanting to be both. Hers is a discourse which questions established cognitive frames in order to open up to the transnational, but never compromises by levelling differences into a partially censored unity. Her voice remains radically revolutionary also after the revolution, as it were, precisely because it goes beyond a simple reversal of established interpretations to dismantle the cognitive foundations of such interpretations. This is evident again in *A Small Place*, where a ten-by-twelve-mile island becomes the focus for understanding global capitalism and in the last section the 'you' and the 'I' of the first part, after being reversed in the second, prismatically blur into mutual 'human beings.' By acknowledging that there are no longer masters to be angry at and consequently slaves to be proud of within the oxymoronic political hegemony of multinational forces, Kincaid addresses the difficult but necessary task of building a cultural discourse capable of accounting for present forms of domination. When Kincaid re-figures the tropical paradise as a 'prison of beauty' and exposes the continuity between colonialism and tourism, she redefines writing as a creolized/queered space capable of accommodating paradox and as an act inextricably linked to survival. Just like cognition that, as an inevitable part of experience, is always elaborated intellectually, Kincaid's writing produces thinking which is at the same time radically propositional and responsively deconstructive.

This responsively deconstructed thinking and the conceptualization of subjectivity it produces are instances of passing identity.[17] Kincaid proposes herself as a passing identity when, at twenty-four years of age, she starts to write and rejects her given name, Elaine Cynthia Potter Richardson to adopt the pen name by which she is known. She rejects a name that carried the mark of a history of slavery and colonialism, and adopts a name that points towards a symbolic rather than a foundational reappropriation of the same history.[18] She chooses Jamaica, not Antigua, as if to underline that her identity is an identification with a cultural space rather than an anchoring to an original place.[19] Kincaid follows the indications of the obeah woman Ma Chess, in *Annie John*, who magically appears and disappears in body and spirit, showing the young protagonist that a 'home' is not a fixed location and giving her the strength to achieve independence, which comes only through separation. Another, more literal form of 'passing' regards the change of domination over Antigua, from the British Empire to US Global Imperialism. Kincaid expands on contemporary imperialism most clearly in *Lucy*, where the separation from the protagonist's mother in Antigua turns into the differently but equally conflictual confrontation with a mother-figure in the US. The passage from one form of domination to another is figured through the queered/creolized relationship between mother and daughter, a space where independence means separation and identification at the same time. Not accidentally, it is in a text fully centred on the mother that Kincaid gives 'passing' the connotation of 'passing for,' rather than 'passing through.'

In *The Autobiography of My Mother*, Xuela exists as an agent because she narrates the autobiography of a woman who is 'becoming her own mother', in order to become herself, birth herself, re-invent herself. Xuela embodies the statement 'my mother is now me,' while celebrating the creativity and continuity of birth as the creative potential to re-define herself.[20] Her personal account imposes itself for its theoretical and thus political value, and it is consequently not surprising that a novel on the mother is dedicated to Derek Walcott rather than to Kincaid's own Dominican mother and Carib Indian grandmother. The dedication takes autobiography out of the personal boundaries and into the realm of cultural production. Compellingly, the loss of one's mother reverberates with the unspeakable suffering of slavery and massacre to dismantle the figuration of the Caribbean as the Other of Europe or the Other America, and allowing instead for it to become a queered/creolized space, created and enriched through speech acts. Kincaid's watchful attention to language is emphasized in *My Garden (Book):*, where metaphors carry the political force of being a cognitive rather than a linguistic entity. This is an exploration of *garden* as an icon for colonial culture: not only as the Garden of Eden but also as England, the Edenic mother country, and the

British Colony as the extension of the English garden; in addition, the botanical garden as history of naming, possessing, classifying, and domesticating large parts of the world; finally, as the image of a feminine confinement in the domestic sphere — the Victorian lady in the garden. As Kincaid herself becomes the gardener, this entire set of associations is responsibly dismantled and the metaphor garden gains a whole new, deeply subversive life, which accepts to be culturally translated through a renunciation strategy, to circulate in different contexts and resists being frozen into a transcendental iconic identity. Its discursive quality retains the rhetoricity of language and works in the silent spaces between and around words, allowing the world to be made of an agent who acts in it in an ethical and political way and, by forcing on us a language that did not previously exist, allows us to queer discourse and to creolize reality.[21] Kincaid's 'decolonialization of language and thought' brings affiliations into a discourse capable of risking language and questioning logic. Knowledge is treated as a cultural elaboration of an experience of suffering and deprivation in *The Autobiography*, *My Brother* and *Mr. Potter*, without seeking resolution through resurrection, redemption, and catharsis — without the need to conquer death.[22] This is evidence that Kincaid's discourse explores the possibilities offered by a thinking which is poetic and historical at the same time and risks not telling us always what we would like to hear but is capable of expressing the hope for a just world.

When *My Brother* elaborates the statement that shapes *At the Bottom of the River* — 'Inevitable to life is death and not inevitable to death is life. Inevitable' — it becomes clear that life for Kincaid is not the opposite of death, but rather includes it. Kincaid's resistance to alterity is expressed also in her refusal to write against death and in so doing to participate in the history of conquest, rape, and inquisitions.[23] Instead, she calls for a re-imagination of our being in the world in the form of a re-birth of epic as arrival, as transfiguration rather than photographic description. Her 'renunciation' strategy transfigures alterity, allowing us to re-think subjectivity as 'a prism, many-sided and transparent, refracting and reflecting light.' Like a Carib Indian flute made of human bone, her music expresses a void which is an inner presence and which her imagination and our listening are invited to fill in unexpected ways.[24] This capacity to express the void has enabled Kincaid to write about the 'nothingness' that is Mr. Potter and break the silence of the subaltern.

To me Kincaid's prism has provided the irreverent inspiration to abuse the words *creole* and *queer* in the attempt to resist confining her work within a single dichotomous frame: the prism absorbs — it is passed through by — the specificity of a materially — grounded creoleness, and it reflects-it passes through — a whole range of multiple, lustrous, rainbow-like colours that only a queer performance of desire can fully express. This multiple function has proved instrumental for my own making sense of our increasingly globalized world.

Notes

1   Jamaica Kincaid with Kathleen M. Balutansky, 'On Gardening' Interview in *Callalloo*, 25:3 (2002): 790-800, p 797.

2   Jamaica Kincaid with Kathleen M. Balutansky, 'On Gardening,' p. 795.

3   As repeated, scattered mentions or implicit references in this study indicate, my reading has been influenced mainly but not exclusively by, alphabetically, Kathy Acker, Gloria Anzaldùa, Liana Borghi, Rosi Braidotti, Angela Carter, Rikki Ducornet, Lorna Goodison, Jessica Hagedorn, Teresa de Lauretis, Audre Lorde, Chandra T. Mohanty, Adrienne Rich, Gayatri C. Spivak, Trinh-Minh-Ha.

4   Gayatri C. Spivak, *A Critique of Postcolonial Reason: Towards a History of the Vanishing Present*, Cambridge: Harvard University Press, 1999, p. 385.

5   Dana Nelson, 'ConsterNation' in Donald E. Pease and Robyn Wiegman, eds., *The Futures of American Studies*, Durham: Duke University Press, 2002: 559-580, pp. 575, 572, 576.

6   William V. Spanos, *America's Shadow*, Minneapolis: Minnesota University Press, 2000, p.192.

7   Jamaica Kincaid with Kathleen M. Balutansky, 'On Gardening', p. 792.

8   Gayatri C. Spivak, *A Critique of Postcolonial Reason*, p. 336.

9   Gayatri C. Spivak, *A Critique of Postcolonial Reason*, p. 383.

10   Elaine Scarry, *On Beauty and Being Just*, Princeton: Princeton University Press; 1999.

11   Liana Borghi, 'Liminaliens and Others-But Mostly Vamps, Dragons and Women' in Giovanna Covi, ed. *Critical Studies on the Feminist Subject*, Trento: Dipartimento di Scienze Filologiche e Storiche, 1997:101-25.

12   Henrik Gottlieb and Yives Gambier, eds., 'Multi Media Translation : Concepts, Practices, and Research' in *Benjamins Translation Library*, V:34: 166-68.

13   For a comprehensive discussion of this meaning of queer in the context of contemporary critical theories, see Mario Corona, ed., *Incroci di genere*, Bergamo: Edizioni Sestante, 1999; Alice Bellagamba, Paola di Cori, and Marco Pustianaz, eds., *Generi di Traverso*, Vercelli: Edizioni Mercurio, 2000.

14   Caryl Phillips, Interview in *Kunapipi*, 11:2 (1989): 44-50.

15   Jack Forbes, *Africans and Native Americans*, Urbana: University of Illinois P, 1993.

16   Edouard Glissant, *Caribbean Discourse*, Charlottesville: University Press of Virginia, 1989; Antonio Benítez-Rojo, *The Repeating Island*, Durham: Duke University Press, 1992.

17   Liana Borghi, 'Introduzione: L'occhio del[l]'ago' in *Passaggi: Letterature comparate al femminile*, Urbino: Quattroventi, 2002.

18   Jamaica Kincaid with Leslie Garis, Interview 'Through West Indian Eyes' in *New York Times Sunday Magazine*, 7 October 1990: 42.

19   On the concept identification, see Diana Fuss, *Identification Papers*, New York: Routledge, 1995 and Donna Haraway, *Simians, Cyborgs and Women*, New York: Routledge, 1991 and *Modest Witness @ Second Millennium FemaleMan Meets Onco Mouse*, New York: Routledge, 1997.

20   Lorna Goodison, *I Am Becoming My Mother*, London: New Beacon, 1986.

21   Gayatri C. Spivak, 'The Politics of Translation' in Michèle Barret and Anne Phillips, eds., *Destabilizing Theory: Contemporary Feminist Debates*, Palo Alto, CA: Stanford University Press, 1992: 177-200; Angela Carter, 'Notes from the Frontline,' in Michelène Wandor, ed., *On Gender and Writing*, London: Pandora, 1983: 69-77.

22   Wilson Harris, 'Quetzalcoatl and the Smoking Mirror (Reflections on Originality and Tradition)' (Address toTemenos Academy, London, 7 February 1994), *The Review of Contemporary Fiction*, 17:2 (Summer 1997): 12-23. p. 22.

23   Wilson Harris, 'Quetzalcoatl and the Smoking Mirror,' p. 18.

24   Wilson Harris, 'Cross-Cultural Crisis: Imagery, Language and the Intuitive Imagination' in *Commonwealth Lectures* 1990 n. 2, Oct. 31, 1990. University of Cambridge.

Index

Nagel, James 96n.46
Nasta, Susheila 63n.9, 96n.46
Nelson, Dana 136, 144n.5
Niesen de Abruna, Laura 63n.9, 74, 95n.23, 108, 132n.31

O'Brien, Susie 26n.45
O'Callaghan, Evelyn 78, 95n.27
O'Connor, Patricia 74, 94n.22
'On Seeing England for the First Time' 14, 47-52, 127
'Ovando' 14, 29, 42-46, 108, 127, 129

Palmer, Opal Adisa 133n.44
Paravisini-Gebert, Lisabeth 63n.9, 69, 73, 94n.11, 94n.19, 130n.1, 133n.35
Philip, Nourbese N. 130n.5
Phillips, Caryl 139, 144n.14
postcolonial discourse 28-30, 31-32, 36, 38, 42, 46, 52, 52-53, 73, 78, 81, 98-101,
        107-108, 110, 111, 125, 127-128,
prismatic subjectivity 8-9, 11, 12, 16-17, 18, 19, 23, 28-30, 33, 49, 50, 52, 57-58, 60,
        61, 62, 72, 80-81, 84-85, 86, 98-101, 116, 117-118, 127, 130, 132n.25
Pynchon, Thomas 39, 65n.16
Pyne Timothy, Helene 73, 94n.17

Ramchad, Kenneth 79, 95n.29
Ray, Saangeta 133n.45
Reckwitz, Erhard, Lucia Vennarini and Cornelia Wegener 95n.28
Réjouis, Rose-Myriam 27n.48
Rhys, Jean 110
Rich, Adrienne, 9, 20, 24n.8, 57, 62n.1, 66n.47, 93n.5, 93n.7, 131n.12, 145n.3

Sackville West, Vita 56
Said, Edward 45, 65n.22, 131n.7
San Juan, Epifanio 65n.14, 99
Sassen, Saskia 66n.48
Scarry, Elaine 9, 24n.10, 129, 134n.57, 134n.58, 145n.10
Schine, Cathleen 131n.16
Scott, Helen 96n.46
Sedgwick, Eve K. 12, 24n.12
Shakespeare, William 90
Shama, Simon 66n.37
Sheenan, Thomas 134n.53
Shelley Wollstonecraft, Mary 91
Schultheis, Alexandra 133n.35
Simmons, Diane 63n.9, 64n.10, 95n.35, 108, 132n.29
Skow, John 134n.46
Smith, Sidonie 81, 85, 87, 93n.1, 95n.32, 95n.33, 106, 132n.24